Recall

A handbook

Research & Education Division
Help the Aged.

Recall – audio/visual sequences researched and produced by Nick Alderton and Carmel Sammons.

Recall – *A handbook* written by Susanna Johnston from material by Carmel Sammons, Nick Alderton and Mick Kemp. Chapter 5: Childhood, Youth, Living through the Thirties written by Eve Hostettler; The Second World War written by Eve Hostettler and Carmel Sammons; The Great War written by Joanna Bornat; A Different World written by Edward Baker and Joanna Bornat.

Graphic Design: Carlos Sapochnik

Photographs: Nick Alderton, Carmel Sammons, Stephen Whaley.

Printed by Unwin Brothers, Woking.

Published by Research & Education Division, Help the Aged, St James's Walk, London EC1R 0BE

Acknowledgements

Help the Aged gratefully acknowledges the following people who generously gave their time, talents and facilities to help the *Recall* project: Mr. Edward Baker, Mrs. Rose Baxter, Dick Busby, Anna Davin, Cathie Edwards, Mr. Edward Fishman, Malcolm Ford and the London Boroughs' Training Committee, Bill Furlong, Thelma Harvey, Mrs. Dorothy Hollingsworth, John Hook, Mick Kemp and the Department of Health and Social Security, Rowena Kinsman, Mr. George MacGregor, Andrew Norris, Mr. Chris Rice, Lindsay Royan and the staff and visitors of the London Hospital: Stepney Day Hospital, Thea Thompson, Les Todd and the Inner London Education Authority, Stephen Whaley and the School of Communications: Polytechnic of Central London, Mrs. Alex Zeitoun and all the many other people who encouraged us with their own enthusiasm.

The project would not have been possible without the very generous help received from the following photographic and sound archives and recording companies: British Film Institute, British Institute of Recorded Sound (Elizabeth Wells), British Museum Newspaper Library, BBC Hulton Picture Library, BBC Sound Archives (Mark Jones), Columbia, Decca Ltd, E.M.I. Ltd., Fox's Photographic Archives, Greater London Council Photograph Library, HMV Ltd, Imperial War Museum, John Topham Picture Library, Kodak Museum, K-Tel, Marylebone Library, Museum of London, Southwark Local Studies Library, United Artists Music Ltd.

Reminiscence Aids Project 1978/1979
Department of Health and Social Security

Team

Mick Kemp	Architect, DHSS, Team Leader
Nick Alderton	Artist, photographer
Ian Breakwell	Artist, writer and film-maker
Hugh Davies	Artist, musician
Bill Furlong	Artist, Audio Arts
Rowan Matthews	Psychologist
Carmel Sammons	Artist, designer
David Toop	Artist, musician
Arre Bekkering	Medical student (visiting)

Advisory Committee

Dr. Gordon Langley	Psychiatrist, Exeter
Dr. Roy Boyd	Geriatrician, Nottingham
Graham Clarke	Community Nursing Officer
Pat Healy	Social Services Journalist, *The Times*
John Hook	Geriatric Hospital Volunteer Organiser, Dulwich
Anne Hansford	BBC film and video library
Mark Jones	BBC Sound Adviser
Lawrence Stapley	BBC Recording Service
Barbara Steveni	APG (Research) Ltd.
Jane Vollans	Psychologist, Institute of Psychiatry
Edward Baker	Retired worker, London

Contents

Reminiscence and Old Age

Recalling the past is something which most of us do, whatever our age, whether on our own or with family or friends. Sometimes we do it deliberately: we may recall the past to help solve present problems, to put things in perspective or to give advice out of our own experience. We may try to resolve past conflicts, problems or griefs by reassessing them in the light of the present. We may remember ourselves in the past, as even quite young children do, to reassure ourselves of our own progress and development.

At other times our recall of the past may be unexpectedly triggered off by an old song, an evocative smell, a forgotten object or picture. We may be talking of past events and find in remembering the specific event we also recall a whole host of personal details and impressions which we thought we had forgotten. Recalling and sharing these memories with others is satisfying and enjoyable.

The older we get the more of our life we have to look back on, the greater the changes we have seen and the more experience we have to reinterpret the past. For these reasons, the memoirs and reminiscences of articulate and distinguished older people are sought after by publishers, television and radio programme makers and the press.

While these recollections are appreciated, the value and significance of the reminiscences of ordinary old people is not always perceived.

In the last decade there has been increasing interest by psychologists and psychogeriatricians in the function of reminiscence. They have seen in this common tendency a 'psychologically healthy form of communication'[1]. The research of Charles N Lewis[2] indicates that the ability to reminisce is in fact not only normal but necessary and desirable. Old people with the ability and inclination to remember their past and relate it to the present appear to have a stronger concept of self and respond with greater self-confidence and less stress when subjected to stress inducing circumstances. Robert Butler[3] has written of the need to review one's life in old age which may be responsible for the increased reminiscence of older people. He postulates the theory that it is this process of life review which contributes both to late-life psychological disorders, particularly to depression, 'and the evolution of such characteristics as candor, serenity and wisdom among certain of the aged.'

But, Butler comments, far from appreciating the function of reminiscence in the aged, the more usual reaction on the part of the listener is to associate it with psychological disfunction and to regard it as a symptom. One of the reasons for this dismissive attitude may well be that research into ageing was until comparatively recently concentrated on samples of elderly people living in institutions and containing a disproportionate number of mentally disordered people. Thus the tendency has been to associate reminiscence predominately with abnormal and pathological patterns of ageing.

However, there is also impatience amongst younger people of the reminiscence of older people who are not mentally disordered: reminiscence is seen as 'living in the past', 'escapism' and so on. Both Butler and Lewis stress the importance of overcoming this impatience and listening to older people. Butler stresses the rewards for the listener: 'The personal sense and meaning of the life cycle are more clearly unfolded by those who have nearly completed it. The nature of the forces shaping one's life, the effects of life events, the fate of neuroses and character disorders, the dénouement of character itself may be studied in the older person. Recognition of the occurrence of a vital process (the life review) may help one to listen, tolerate and understand the aged and not to treat reminiscence as devitalised and insignificant.'

The influence of the work of Butler, Lewis and others[4] in this field has been crucial in the development of Recall. So, too, has the kind of rehabilitative work with elderly mental patients described by James C Folsom.[5] The starting point for this work in America in the early 1960's was a realisation that although the physical needs of elderly mental patients were being well met, the emotional needs of individual patients required concentrated attention. Fifty elderly psychiatric patients were living on the ward in a totally protected environment with intensive nursing attention. The patients were allowed to do almost nothing for themselves for fear they might fall and be hurt. Fourteen of the fifty patients spent most of their time in wheelchairs. The injury rate and intercurrent illness rate among the patients was very high.

A programme of activities was devised and implemented with the patients by the Rehabilitative Team. A feature of the programme was a recognition of the key role of the nursing assistants (auxiliaries) in planning and carrying out activities with the patients under the supervision of the appropriate therapists. Ten patients left their wheelchairs permanently.

'The small group activities focused on involving patients with the environment and with other human beings. Soon there was an air of liveliness throughout the unit. Patients and personnel were anxious to complete the daily toileting and . . . duties as quickly as possible so they could get on with more interesting activities . . . The patients began conversing and making friends . . . There was a most surprising change in the attitude of the employees towards the geriatric patients. Instead of personnel shunning this unit, there was a waiting list of people who wanted to transfer to (it).'

The second part of Folsom's paper describes the application to geriatric mental patients of reality orientation techniques originally devised for younger, acute mental patients. 'We considered each patient carefully to find areas of *wellness*', says Folsom. 'When we found such an area, we tried to expand its boundaries.'

Reality orientation therapy with elderly patients has been developed in this country by Una Holden and Alex Sinebruchow in Leeds and in their paper[6] they list among the techniques the use of 'pictures and mementos of the two World Wars . . . Film, photographs, models or antiques . . . Basic to the therapy is the need to capitalise on the patients' long-term memory stores.'

This then is the clinical and therapeutic context of *Recall* – the recognition of the psychological function of reminiscence, the relatively recent appreciation that there were 'areas of wellness' in psychogeriatric patients which would respond to intensive care and a new conviction that progress and rehabilitation for institutionalised elderly patients is possible.

There is also the growing awareness that programmes of treatment must take into account the total needs of older people. J Sanbourne Bockoven has written[7] of the especial vulnerability of the elderly patient who has been 'exposed to wear and tear and stresses and strains for the greatest length of time . . . Elderly individuals are in varying degrees *displaced persons*, i.e., strangers in their own families and communities largely as a result of rapid socio-economic changes which took place during the latter half of their lives and for which many had little opportunity to prepare. A number of these people live in desolation. They are the casualties of the social forces which have dislocated their habitual way of life. Many of them may not be in need of medical attention.' He concludes that there is a need to discover common ground both between the various disciplines desiring to serve the older generation better and greater social solidarity between the generation of elders and their descendants.

Recall attempts to create in some degree that common ground and to help lessen those feelings of 'dislocation' which some of our elderly people experience.

In parallel with this growing psychological and sociological awareness the last decade has seen, too, a groundswell of interest in oral history. Universities, colleges, evening classes, neighbourhood groups, local history groups and schools are going into the community with tape-recorders or setting up workshops to learn from each other about the past. The function of history in enabling people to understand their own situation and the upheavals and transformations which they have witnessed in their past has become widely recognised.

Paul Thompson[8] emphasises the social uses of oral history in breaking down barriers and in democratising history: 'It can break down barriers between teachers and students, between generations, between educational institutions and the world outside; and in the writing of history – whether in books, or museums, or radio and film – it can give back to the people who made and experienced history, through their own words, a central place.'

In the same way that the pursuit of oral history demands the breaking of conventional boundaries between professional historians and the ordinary public, *Recall* requires the laying aside of professional roles in the sphere of social welfare and institutional care. For despite its potential in a total therapeutic programme, *Recall* is not itself a therapy but a way of establishing a collaboration – either a collaboration of contemporaries, eager to relive common experiences of the past and to recall and share their own unique experiences, or a collaboration of 'staff' and 'clients', young and old, in a process of mutual discovery.

Just as oral history encourages a reinterpretation of the past based on the experiences of ordinary people, so the stimulation and discussion of the reminiscence and life experience of older 'patients' or 'clients' may lead to a re-evaluation of their needs as individuals with respect to their treatment and environment.

The communication of reminiscence happens naturally for those who live surrounded by family and friends. But with changing social patterns older people may find themselves increasingly isolated. Sometimes they may be totally separated from familiar points of reference (physical, mental and emotional) on admission to a home, hospital or other institution. As a consequence, deprived of the traditional stimuli and incentives to reminisce, the old may end up existing in a social and personal vacuum. Apathy, confusion and mental decline are often responses to feelings of anonymity.

There is an increasing awareness amongst staff in homes and hospitals of the importance of creating a stimulating environment for older people including those suffering from confusion or dementia and of the need to involve patients and residents in activities. Much good work is being done by adult educators coming into institutions to teach art, music, keep-fit etc.[9] Research has shown the positive effects of various psychological and social interventions on groups of patients and residents.[10]

What appears to be important is to increase and maintain the level of social stimulation. The day to day role of the permanent caring staff is therefore very important. But there are difficulties which need to be recognised. The demands of caring for the physical needs of the elderly may be very time consuming; staff may be in short supply; the staff may see their role as 'carers' in the sense of keeping their clients safe, clean and fed or as nurses to provide medical care; the environment of the institution may be unsympathetic; the staff may be unaware of the difference that a more stimulating environment could make to patients or residents who appear totally apathetic or confused; there may be a fear of 'getting involved' or being bored; there may be a simple lack of resources.

One of the aims in producing *Recall* was to stimulate the imagination of the 'carers' as well as the memories of the older participants and to provide an easily used tool to encourage and maintain communication.

Recall provides a common frame of reference, a focus and it invites a unique response from each individual.

It can introduce an element of reality into the 'unreal' world of the institution and build a bridge between the institution and the world outside. Volunteers and professionals, young and old, family and friends can all be involved either in showing the programmes or contributing memories, souvenirs and objects which can transform a sterile, impersonal environment into a place of shared memories and cultural and intellectual significance.

The History of Recall

Recall began as The Reminiscence Aids Project in the Department of Health and Social Security[1]. In 1976, Mick Kemp as architectural adviser on accommodation for the elderly mentally infirm, circulated a paper on the subject and in 1977/78 applied for research funds to produce Reminiscence Aids and carry out field tests of their effectiveness. Reminiscence Aids were defined as 'an audio-visual method of stimulating reminiscence in elderly people, including those with mental infirmity.' They were to consist of photographic slides covering specific periods within the lifetime of people currently aged between 75 and 100, accompanied by a tape sound-track of appropriate music, spoken material and sound effects. In the original conception there was to be a presentation for each year since 1900 but practical considerations led to a decision to attempt to produce one presentation for each decade since 1900 with special coverage for each of the two world wars.

It had also been intended that the target group of elderly people should include hospital patients with severe mental infirmity, but once again practical considerations arising from early trials led to this group being ruled out and presentations were aimed at the less severely mentally infirm or confused elderly people largely living in Part III accommodation.

From the outset the team[2] envisaged Reminiscence Aids as a means of helping someone talk to individual old people, or groups, about their memories, although it was also recognised that mentally alert older people might also enjoy looking at the presentations on their own. The team hoped in addition to providing mental stimulation that Reminiscence Aids would:

a) provide a framework for caring interaction between old people, care and nursing staff and others.

b) by evoking reminiscence in the presence of an interested listener, restore a sense of personal value to the older person.

c) enable old people to regain a fuller perspective of their own past lives, the better to relate to the present.

These were some of the long term benefits which the team hoped would arise out of a successful Reminiscence Aids programme. The short term objectives of the one year study were set down as the following:

(i) to demonstrate that an apparatus using photographic slides and tape recorded sound[3] could be produced which would increase reminiscence in the elderly with mental infirmity.

(ii) that such an apparatus would have recreational benefits for the elderly.

From the outset it was decided that it should be the reminiscence of the elderly themselves which would determine the content of the slide/tape sequences, rather than any systematic or 'objective' view of the past. The basic criterion for the inclusion of any photograph or sound would be the amount of reminiscence or discussion which it provoked. There would be no attempt to cover impartially historically significant episodes or trends.

It was decided that the sequences should reflect working class conditions in London and have a slight bias towards women, since in this age group they are numerically greater.

With these basic terms of reference having been agreed, the following measures were rapidly put in hand:

(i)   visits were made to selected establishments for the elderly with mental infirmity. A variety of photographs from each decade was shown to residents in an attempt to gauge the likely effect on memory of photographic images where these were not personally connected with the individual.

(ii) Approaches were made to London radio stations and the BBC for help in appealing for reminiscences of the period from elderly listeners.

(iii) An advisory commmittee[4] was set up with representatives from geriatric medicine, psychiatry, psychology, journalism, BBC sound and television archives, nursing and voluntary workers, who kindly agreed to participate by acting as advisers and critics during the project.

The visits with the photographs gave early indications that photographic images could indeed evoke memory even where the subject matter was not personally connected with the individual. It soon became obvious that memories of common experiences could be triggered off by a single image or sound and that once the common experience had been discussed, there were many individual anecdotes which sprang from it. It also became apparent that certain subjects consistently failed to produce the same level of response or degree of intensity in reminiscence. Generally, subjects which related closely to the home and the immediate street environment proved most effective in stimulating recall and reminiscence.

The appeal to radio stations led to a short series of broadcasts on BBC Radio London which in turn led to further broadcasts and articles which brought letters from elderly people giving invaluable recollections.

The first complete presentation, that covering World War II, was ready in August 1978 and was used to test the principle of Reminiscence Aids. The presentation consisted of 60 slides and lasted about 18 minutes. It was shown to a variety of elderly audiences and amendments were made following comments from audiences on its evocative power. Lessons were learnt, too, about methods of talking to elderly people during and after viewing. In addition, an early fear that reference to the war years might upset or frighten elderly people was largely dispelled, although it remained policy throughout that no person thought likely to be disturbed would be invited to see such a presentation.

The results from the World War II presentation were sufficiently encouraging to justify work on further presentations and sequences on 1920's, 1930's and World War I were completed. As an experiment into the possible effect of subject-related rather than chronologically-related presentations on memory, a presentation on 'Childhood' was prepared. This sought, through images and sounds from all ages and conditions of childhood taken from each of the decades, to evoke memories in the minds of the elderly from one of the periods in their lives when childhood would have affected them: their own childhood, parenthood, grandparenthood. There was not time to carry out full field trials on this presentation, but early indications were that women who had had children of their own responded to the presentation, since it seemed to be parent and grandparenthood which was evoked rather than personal childhood.

A further presentation, produced specifically for use with elderly severely mentally infirm patients, was produced. This was based on the original World War II presentation but with fewer and simpler images and sounds and paced more slowly. This was tested with patients at a London psychiatric hospital. Although this sequence was not extensively tested, earlier trials had shown that certain people responded increasingly in proportion to the number of times they saw the presentation. However, the work involved in procuring such responses was beyond the resources of the team. This experience was of major importance in the decision to concentrate on the less severely confused elderly.

As each of the presentations was completed, it was checked for impact with groups of confused and alert elderly people and modified as necessary. It was the reminiscences of the alert elderly which proved invaluable in determining the direction of the research into pictures and sounds. One particularly interested correspondent[5] was co-opted on to the Advisory Committee.

In 1979 a formal testing programme was devised[6] and carried out under strict controlled conditions. Each of the sequences was shown, on a one-to-one basis, to pre-selected groups of elderly people in four Part III homes, after which they were asked the same set of questions. An attempt was made to measure any increase in reminiscence by judging the quality of the reply and setting it down on a four point scale. The results of the testing were sent for statistical analysis but failed to produce figures which could be regarded as proof that the sequences were in fact responsible for any increase in reminiscence. Psychometric measurement is probably inadequate to the task of recording the reactions which the team witnessed during the interviews. The very act of questioning served to inhibit response and conceal reactions which had clearly happened moments before the questions were asked. Many of these reactions were non-verbal, varying from evident visual engagement to foot-tapping and nodding to tunes, silent mouthing of words and smiles and nods of recognition as images and sounds materialised.

The team were able to note some of these reactions on paper and the interviews were tape-recorded and show that there was an immediate, spontaneous response. But neither of these techniques can adequately express what was evident to the observers at the time, which was that reminiscence was clearly being stimulated by the presentation and that the majority of elderly people evidently enjoyed what they had seen. One further point of interest was that evidence from one of the homes showed that there had been a noticeable change in behaviour in two residents in the days following the second round of presentations. One woman had resumed using make-up and caring for her appearance and a man had regained interest in his wartime experiences. In both cases the staff had accepted years of self-neglect as an irreversible decline.

The failure of this attempt to subject the effects of Reminiscence Aids to rigorous scientific analysis may be partly due to the fact that the study did not select appropriate areas for analysis. The study was not designed to record any modifications in behaviour of the subjects over a period of time. It was also unable to gauge the degree of non-verbal reminiscence and emotional response.

Reminiscence Aids was, from its conception, an arts-based project. Originated by an architect, the project also had the support of a member of the Artists' Placement Group[7] who was working at that time in the DHSS. They brought together a team which consisted mainly of artists and musicians. Apart from an inbuilt awareness of the appearance of the environment an artist is also trained in specific techniques of communication and accustomed to registering the effects of visual and aural images on others. Artists are used to working without firm preconceptions or 'rules', using their imaginations and a process of trial and error in developing their work. Their perceptions may lead them to make connections which are those of the imagination rather than of logic and to experiment with unexpected combinations to evoke responses. The field which the Reminiscence Aids team was working in was one hitherto regarded as the province of doctors, psychologists and psychogeriatricians. While the team was aware of the work done by people in these disciplines and of current scientific theories of how memory functions, they did not approach this project as scientists but as artists and communicators. The project enabled the artists to apply their training in the use of various media and their innate qualities and perceptions to a new field. It also provided the opportunity for an original collaboration between artists and the psychiatrists, psychologists, therapists and geriatricians.

By August 1979 six sequences had been produced and the final testing had been carried out and the report on the project written. The team had also experimented with putting up exhibitions of large black and white photographs in day centres and psychogeriatric wards. These were accompanied by displays of objects and ephemera. A great amount had been learnt by the team and the advisory committee about the development and application of Reminiscence Aids. A second stage of the project had been planned: the further refinement and testing of the existing sequences and the production of regional sets which could be tested by people outside the team in a variety of settings. There were however no further funds available in the DHSS.

Help the Aged Education Department was invited to take over the project and the two researchers, Carmel Sammons and Nick Alderton, agreed to continue work on the project under the Director of the Education Department.

The new team started work in September 1980. By this time there was considerable interest in the idea of using Reminiscence Aids amongst a wide variety of people who had learnt about it through articles in the press[8] and radio[9] and TV[10] programmes or seeing the presentations demonstrated at conferences or during field trials.

It seemed at this stage that the most important thing was to publish the sequences in a practical and inexpensive format and to encourage people to use them as core material and as a model for developing their own presentations. It also seemed important to pass on the valuable practical experience which the team had gained in working with Reminscence Aids in various settings. The sequences and the results of the research and the original criteria for the selection of material were reviewed with this objective in mind. As a result there were several changes in approach.

An independent study[11] had indicated that Reminscence Aids could be very useful in training programmes for care staff and nursing officers working with the elderly. It therefore seemed important that the presentations should be interesting and entertaining for a wide audience, not just elderly people suffering from mental infirmity. But the especial needs of this last group were also carefully considered.

The new team decided to cut down the number of slides to twenty in each set to enable each picture to remain on the screen for a longer time. This meant that the image could be properly assimilated in detail and overall atmosphere.

In the earlier presentations the sound track was fairly independent of the pictures. It was decided that the sound track should wherever possible reinforce the visual image. The exceptions to this occur when it was not possible to find the appropriate sound or image, or where one or the other was felt to be sufficient on its own.

Since there were to be fewer slides, in order to keep important topics covered there would be more recorded speech and reminiscence in the final presentations. This, it was recognised, would not always be heard or assimilated by confused older people or those who are hard of hearing. However trials revealed that it was useful in encouraging the audience to contribute their own reminiscences, since it made the presentation seem more informal.

Rather than rigidly organising the material into decades, it was decided to organise the material around significant periods in the lives of the elderly. This organisation matches more closely the way people remember the past. It was also considered important to produce a final sequence which related the past to the present and would encourage evaluation of the past, comparisons with the present and discussion of contemporary issues.

Finally there was the problem of location to resolve. It was decided that since *Recall*, as the project was named by Help the Aged, was to be primarily a model, it would be more satisfactory to keep the images and reminiscences to a single geographic location and to make no attempt to represent regional or indeed class differences. There would however be much visual material in all the sequences which was general since it was based on universal experiences of childhood, domestic routine, war time and so on. The music and broadcasts, too, would have a national significance.

These then were the terms of reference for the six new sequences which were produced for publication. There is still work to be done in evaluating the effects on the elderly confused – particularly those living in institutions – of stimulating reminiscence. Is there a case for considering more reminiscence-based activity in therapy for the elderly mentally infirm? The next stage in the history of *Recall* will be determined by those who use these sequences and develop further presentations which reflect local conditions and interest.

Using Recall

Introduction to the six sequences

Recall is divided into three parts. Each part contains two sequences (each consisting of a 12 minute tape and 20 slides) which roughly correspond to periods in the lives of our elderly people. The material for each part reflects the perspective of someone now about 80 years old.

Part I: Childhood and The Great War, assumes that memories of 'childhood' would relate to the years between 1903 and 1913. During the 1914-18 War a man or woman now aged 80 would have been 13-17.

In Part II: Youth and Living through the Thirties, the first sequence concentrates on the years after the First World War – that time when our audience were finding their first job and courting. Living through the Thirties focuses on aspects of life relevant to young couples building a home and rearing families at a time of national depression and unemployment.

In Part III: The Second World War is presented from the view point of men and women who would have been in their late thirties and middle forties coping with young families, war work and air raids at home and fighting overseas. The final sequence, A Different World, looks at some of the major social changes which older people have seen in their lifetime and provides some ways in to discussion about present life and attitudes and comparisons with the past. This is particularly valuable if the sequences have been shown chronologically and earlier reminiscence can be related to present day issues. Conversely younger participants will have something with which to compare their own experience, attitudes and values.

The images have been selected for their power to evoke reminiscence in a group of people. They are designed to act as 'triggers' to memory and not to provide a 'potted history'.

Such short programmes cannot hope to cover more than a few aspects of each period but where the omissions are noticed by the audience, these topics by their very absence serve as stimuli to reminiscence, discussion and controversy.

While in most cases people have come to terms with the sad episodes in their lives some may weep, perhaps for the first time, remembering a past grief which they have suppressed for years. One woman wrote of the 'blessed relief' in releasing this emotion. She added however that the staff around her became very concerned when she cried.

	1900	1914	1920	1930	1939	1950	1960	1970	1980
Born in									
1880	20	34	40	50	59	70	80	90	100
1885	15	29	35	45	54	65	75	85	95
1890	10	24	30	40	49	60	70	80	90
1895	5	19	25	35	44	55	65	75	85
1900		**14**	**20**	**30**	**39**	**50**	**60**	**70**	**80**
1905		9	15	25	34	45	55	65	75
1910		4	10	20	29	40	50	60	70
1915			5	15	24	35	45	55	65
1920				10	19	30	40	50	60

This chart is a useful, quick reference for establishing the age of older people at various points in this century.

It is perhaps a fact that some younger people and professionals caring for the old wish to protect them overmuch from emotional upset. But there is comfort and strength to be derived from talking over past griefs in a supportive and sympathetic atmosphere with people who may have had similar experiences. Many older people take a pride or sombre satisfaction in recalling the dangers and emotional upheavals which they have survived.

Background information

All the sequences are accompanied by basic background information about the period, notes on the slides and sounds and suitable prompts or 'cue' questions to help get discussion going. The notes and background information are intended as an aid for the presenters or leaders of groups to help orientate them to periods and circumstances with which they may be totally unfamiliar. Some preparation beforehand enables the presenter to approach the experiences of a group of people who may be much older with a basis for understanding. It can also prevent the leader feeling 'left out' once the discussion really takes off. But it is not the role of the group leader to be an expert – indeed a degree of ignorance provided it is accompanied by a genuine interest is often a good thing in bolstering the confidence of the group members and drawing out more reminiscence and information.

Cue questions

The 'cue' questions are simply a guide to help presenters get discussion going and should not in any way be regarded as a questionnaire to be worked through methodically (to see how much attention the audience has been paying!). They tend to focus the discussion on areas of shared common experience which allow everyone to join in without fear of having to reveal intimacies or to become embarrassed because they cannot remember much. The presenter may well wish to abandon them in favour of questions which arise from natural curiosity or personal interest. It may be that after showing one of the sequences, a discussion arises which does not relate specifically to the period just depicted. It is not important that the conversations which arise from the programme should always relate to them. Memory frequently works by association and does not record or submit memories in chronological order. It is as well to be prepared, therefore, for a discussion to revolve around many different topics without feeling that the session has been spoilt or that the 'purpose' has been lost.

As the session develops general discussion about common experiences may well give way to more personal recollections. These personal anecdotes may form the basis of one-to-one discussions at a later date between members of the group with or without

the group leader and in some cases may be common ground for forming deeper relationships. It is therefore important to try and remember any little personal details that have arisen during the group discussion, for example, what job Mrs. X said she used to do before she got married.

Setting up the equipment and showing the programmes

Make sure that everyone knows what it is they are invited to watch and give people enough time to gather together in a relaxed way. If the presentation is to take place in a day centre, home or hospital make sure that the timing doesn't clash with meals or coffee breaks.

The group may be any size. A large group, twenty or thirty, gives the occasion more excitement – a smaller group, twelve or so, may make for a more intimate discussion.

Depending on the number of people in the group, and on the equipment which is available, the programmes can be shown using front or back projection. With front projection a large image can be projected on to a screen or a blank wall. With back projection a T.V. sized image is projected on to a small screen built into the projector. The lights will need to be dimmed but not always necessarily turned off as this can be a little unnerving for some elderly people. It is a good idea to keep the period of darkness to a minimum.

Make sure that everyone is seated so that they have a clear view of the screen. The volume may need to be adjusted to take account of any members of the group who may be hard of hearing.

Despite the simplicity of the programmes there is a good deal to take in from the 12 minute tape and 20 slides and certainly nothing will be lost in repeating the programme either during the same session or at a later date. It is, however, a good idea only to show one sequence per session. Generally it is best to show the entire sequence without interruption the first time, noting any comments and reactions (such as feet tapping to tunes or singing along with songs etc.) While the sequence is in progress it is not necessary that everyone keeps quiet. Sometimes members of the group will tell others to do so and it is probably best to let the group arrive at an understanding between themselves.

The slide/tape format makes it possible for individual slides which created particular interest to be shown again, independently of the sound-track and for an image to be held on the screen for as long as it is wanted. Similarly the tape can be played separately and of course stopped at any point for discussion. It can also be used entirely on its own for the benefit of people who cannot see well or who are blind.

Some people tire sooner than others and it is as well to bring the session to an end while people still have something to say rather than letting the discussion gradually peter out into silence. People who wish will continue to talk to each other and the group as a whole will look forward to another session.

The role of the presenter

The role of the presenter will vary depending on the group but there are a few general points to bear in mind. There is above all a need really to listen to what people say and to take an interest in their individual experiences while ensuring that all the members of the group who wish (and some may prefer to say nothing) get the chance to contribute. The presenter needs to understand and respect the views of the group, even when he or she does not share the opinions expressed.

To get discussion going, it is best to start with open-ended questions which invite reminiscence on general topics – preferably picking up a point made by someone in the group in response to a picture or sound. Questions which require the recall of specific pieces of information such as names or dates should be avoided – at any rate initially. In many cases discussion will break out spontaneously but it is as well to have one or two questions ready in case people are shy.

If any slide generates particular interest, return to it and put it up on the screen. If a piece of music seems to get feet tapping, play it again and ask questions about the memories it brings back. Music is often a powerful evoker of exact memories of time and place.

General discussion may well start with people reinforcing each other's opinions but discussions can become lively! The presenter's job may be to ask a provocative question to 'ginger' things up or, alternatively, tactfully to introduce new elements into a debate which is becoming limited to a few in the group to the exclusion of others. Different groups will set their own pace – some may like a leisurely unfolding of memories – so there is no need to be embarrassed by silence or pauses while people reflect on what they have seen or heard. Much reminiscence may be internal and private. A light remark can help the silence from becoming oppressive.

Follow-up activities

It adds immediacy and variety to the discussion to have back-up materials which people can handle and pass around. These might include photographs from albums, scrapbooks, articles from newspapers or magazines, objects such as washboards, bars of Sunlight washing soap or blue bag which evoke through sight, smell and touch the old wash day routine, or marbles, old cigarette cards and comics which bring back memories of childhood.

The above photograph led to a conversation about the remembered perils of the old fashioned mangle. One member of the group showed a scar on a middle finger – the result of getting her finger nipped in the roller when she was a child. Several members of the group immediately showed middle fingers with identical scars – produced in the same way!

The reminiscences and interests of the group will suggest other ideas. The group might like to put their own exhibition together or record their reminiscence either on tape or in writing – perhaps making a programme or a book which would give pleasure to others outside the group.

One group of people attending a Day Centre in the East End of London recalled how as children they used to make a 'grotto' on the outside wall of a house out of paper and cigarettes cards and other bits and pieces. They recreated this on the wall of a day centre and one man demonstrated how they would ask for pennies for this from the men returning from work. The impromptu performance in which all the group participated ended in much laughter. It would be interesting to know whether this tradition was peculiar to the East End or if older people in other parts of the country remember doing something similar.

Using Recall with confused elderly people

In the early stages of the project a slide/tape sequence on the Second World War was shown to severely mentally infirm people in hospital wards with a certain degree of success.[1] The final sequences have not been specially designed with this group in mind and there have been no resources available for testing them but some valuable experience was gained from the earlier trials which is set down here for others to build on.

It is important to site the back projection unit or screen in a place which is away from the noise and interference of the main ward but not in a place which is unfamiliar to the patients. It should be a place where patients are accustomed to go as a matter of course and where they do not feel disorientated or claustrophobic. Blacking out the whole ward may well be seen by staff and patients as a complete disruption of routine.

It is a good idea to know in advance the ward routine and to time the presentation so that it does not coincide with a period when people are distracted by something else. For instance, half an hour before tea time the thought uppermost in most patients' minds may be: 'Tea's coming up.'

Consider the possibility of being on the ward for a long period of time – perhaps from early in the morning until bed-time to show the sequences several times over.

It is best to show the sequences (using a small back projection unit) to one patient at a time. In this way very slight responses, perhaps no more than a slight flexing of the muscles, can be observed and encouraged. If the sequences are shown to a group of patients it may be difficult to listen to any one patient if several conversations break out spontaneously. It is also difficult to return to images or sounds which evoke a response from one person without others becoming bored or agitated.

If the screen is placed so that patients can come or go as they please, some may like to come back and watch the sequences again. In one case which the team observed, an elderly man, Joe, suffering from confusion, came back seven or eight times to watch the presentation. He would sit down behind the people who were showing the programme and during the repeat performances he would chat to the nursing officer and member of the project team. At first there was no indication that the presentation stimulated any extra reminiscence. Joe was asked more or less the same questions repeatedly and almost invariably gave the same answer, 'I don't remember, it was a long time ago.' At one point however, having seen the sequences several times, his range of memory seemed to improve. Having previously seemingly been unable to remember anything about air-raids or shelters, he suddenly answered the question, 'What were the air-raid shelters like?' with the direct answer: 'Very crowded.'

This experience seems to indicate that repeated exposure to the sequences may be helpful in extending the scope of reminiscence in some very confused elderly people, although the response may be due to the continual questioning, general conversation and activity which surrounds the presentation. In any case, Joe was sufficiently interested by the sequence to watch it many times, at several points putting on his glasses to study a particular slide and remarking on something in it. Other patients, more severely mentally impaired and less verbally coherent, responded in other ways. One patient started to write on a piece of paper, unintelligibly – although the words were recognisable. Another who hardly used to move at all seemed to respond with a flexing of the muscles.

It is perhaps important to recognise that much of the response from patients may be internal and almost imperceptible to the presenter. It could for example simply be a fixing of the gaze on one image for a longer period of time. This does not mean that the response is any the less valuable.

Much more work needs to be done on selecting images for the severely mentally impaired. Knowing the individual patients' backgrounds would be very helpful. It could be that the images should be very simple – perhaps details from photographs – so that there are not too many things to look at at once. It may be necessary to have fewer images and to hold each one on the screen longer.

It is important that someone sits beside the patient to pick up the responses and listen to what the patient has to say. It might be a good idea to involve members of the patient's family here, as they would know the patient's background and experience intimately and might understand a response which an 'outsider' would find unintelligible.

The project team also mounted an exhibition in a ward for the severely mentally infirm. The exhibition was the result of collaboration with active elderly people attending a day centre in the same catchment area as the hospital. In the day room of the ward large photographs from the early 1900's were mounted on the walls and a table held games and ephemera which related to childhood and the wash-day routine in the years before the First World War.

Staff, patients and relatives enjoyed talking about the photographs and finding out how the various objects were used. One elderly man gave the team an interesting piece of information about a photograph of a woman using a wash-tub: the tub, he said, was the bottom half of a beer barrel. He knew this because his father used to make them. This anecdote highlights an important principle of Recall – that it enables elderly people, even those who are severely

confused, to give back something to the people who care for them. In situations where older people are dependent and frequently passive recipients, Recall helps create a greater equality between 'staff' and 'clients'. When the exhibition was taken away to another ward, it was missed by both staff and patients.

Using Recall in training

In an independent pilot study[2] of the use of Recall in Part III homes, the researchers examined the interaction between participating residents and care staff. They aimed to determine the usefulness of the sequences as part of a training programme for residential care staff.

They noted: 'Initially the project was greeted with slight apprehension by the care staff but by the conclusion of the trial it was their unanimous opinion that the programme had helped them to understand the different eras through which the residents had lived.'

The study was perhaps most useful in indicating the role the sequences could play as a training aid for care staff in residential homes for the elderly. The researchers noted a high degree of shared enjoyment between staff and residents. They felt the programmes could increase understanding and communication between care staff and residents. The care staff may have no idea of the kind of experiences which the residents have lived through, particularly if they come from different ethnic backgrounds.

The researchers were also aware of the emotional isolation experienced by many residents on admission to a residential home. With all familiar landmarks removed it is not surprising that many residents cling to their armchairs in the lounge and sink into apathy: 'Worried staff can and do try to stimulate residents but all activities such as bingo, crafts, outings stem from the staff and are done to or for the residents. If there is little response staff naturally become discouraged and think that the effort is not worthwhile.' Recall depends on the knowledge of the residents and in telling staff about their own lives they can regain their own self-esteem and begin to develop an understanding from which companionship may develop.

Emphasising the fact that the sequences in Recall were put together on the advice of elderly people can help to make training more lively: older people are seen as individuals who have lived through very different times from our own. Learning something about the past as seen through the eyes of the old themselves, staff, at the very least, can reach a new tolerance and understanding of the reminiscence of the old – if not an active appreciation and respect for their endurance.

The researchers suggest that as part of their training care staff may like to start to develop a collection of photographs and objects which reflect local history. Other suggestions made by training personnel who saw the sequences[3] included the idea of asking staff to put together some photos and objects which would relate to their own lives. This would be particularly interesting if the care staff came from ethnic backgrounds which were unfamiliar to the residents.

Volunteer organisers have also used *Recall* with success. One organiser working in a geriatric ward enlisted the help of the relatives of the patients in preparing an exhibition of objects. One notable result of this project was that the relatives tended to visit the patients more frequently as they became involved in the development of the exhibition.

Recall and school children

Teachers,[4] too, have considered that the sequences have potential for their pupils. They could usefully form part of the training of young volunteers working with the elderly and young people might like to show the presentations in the course of their work or make their own sequences with the help of old people living locally. It is often difficult at first for youngsters to know what to talk to older people about – *Recall* provides a good ice-breaker.

Conclusion

While the prime justification for showing *Recall* in clubs, day centres, residential homes and hospitals must, above all, be the evident enjoyment it creates, the experience of people who have used the sequences indicates that it is more than just entertainment. Not only are the sequences useful in helping groups of older people to get to know each other, they can also promote interaction and communication between staff and clients and help people from younger age groups and different ethnic backgrounds to understand more about the kind of lives older people have lived. The sequences have helped establish communication with confused elderly people.

There is endless scope to develop the ideas in the sequences in the form of exhibitions and displays which involve a number of people in different ways. When these are set up in wards and homes they add interest to the environment, provide opportunities for conversation and interaction and act as incentives for patients or residents to move around and handle objects. There are also opportunities to use *Recall* in conjunction with other therapies.

But perhaps the most important reason for showing *Recall* is that it enables older people who may be living in surroundings or circumstances in which they feel at a disadvantage to regain a feeling of self-esteem. *Recall* not only encourages older people to remember but also to feel pride in the fact that their reminiscence is valued by others as the record of an individual's experience of a long and varied life.

Technical information

The basic equipment you will need to show *Recall* is a cassette tape recorder and a 35mm slide projector, preferably with a carousel or magazine into which you can place all the slides at once. A screen is not necessary if you have a blank wall. If you are using this equipment you will need the version of the tape which is *audibly bleeped*. You will need to ensure in advance that the room can be darkened sufficiently.

To operate:
1. Put the slides into the carousel or magazine.
2. Switch on the projector and advance until the title slide (1) is on the screen. Focus the projector.
3. Insert the cassette into the cassette tape recorder with the title label on the outside. Switch on and check that the cassette is fully rewound.
4. When you are ready, press the *Play* switch on the tape recorder and at the first audible bleep, advance the next slide (2).
Note: Advance the slides exactly at each signal as the sequences are carefully synchronised.

Synchronised equipment

If you have equipment where the projector is electronically linked to a cassette tape recorder you can use the *pulsed version* of the cassette tapes. This means that the slides will be advanced automatically by a silent electronic pulse on the cassette. The tapes are pulsed to a frequency of 1Khz and 150Hz mixed. These pulse frequencies should accommodate *most* machines – but you will need to check the frequency of your own machine.

If you have a machine which has an inbuilt small screen, you will be able to choose whether to project the slides on to this screen – *back projection* – or on to a wall or large screen – *front projection*. With *back projection* the slides are placed in the carousel facing the opposite way from *front projection*.

To operate:
1. Place the loaded slide carousel or magazine into the projector.
2. Switch on the projector and advance until the title slide (1) is on the screen. Focus the projector.
3. Insert the cassette into the cassette player. Switch on and check that the cassette is fully rewound.
4. Play the cassette – the slides will advance automatically.

Getting equipment

There are various places you can try to borrow equipment. The training section of the local Social Services Department, Health Education Officers, Health Clinics, Community Associations, schools, colleges, teacher centres, libraries, local societies, charities, churches or individuals may be prepared to lend projectors or tape recorders.

Most Part III homes and hospitals have amenities funds – a slide projector would make a good addition to a residential home's recreational facilities.

Developing Recall

While being a complete presentation in itself, *Recall* is also a model on which similar programmes geared to specific regions or towns can be based. You may wish to make your own audio-visual sequence or supplement the images and sounds of *Recall* with local photographs and objects.

If you do this, you will want to involve the group as fully as possible both in conversation and by asking for contributions of all kinds to the project. Some additional research may need to be carried out by staff, volunteers, relatives, school children and active members of the group. When you are researching material try and form as accurate a picture in your mind as is possible of the lives of the people in the group so that you recognise the material which will be successful in triggering common memories.

Finding material locally to make audio-visual presentations or exhibitions is not hard. The first resource is, of course, the older people in the group or community who may well have photographs, objects and ephemera which they would be willing to lend. Many people keep a scrap book or a collection of mementos which remind them of the important periods of their lives – school certificates, ration books, magazines. These are primarily of value for their personal associations but may well have wider significance and help to bring back memories of experiences shared by others of their age group.

High days and holidays will probably be well documented: births, christenings, weddings, outings, trips and so on. But other seemingly more mundane areas of life such as employment, housework, shopping etc., are unlikely to have been photographed yet may yield an equally rich source of objects and ephemera. Attics or cupboards may hold flat irons, washboards, gas masks, old magazines and forgotten childhood collections of postcards, cigarette cards and so on.

Other sources of material are shops and local industries which may have photographs of the work place and the work force. They may be able to allow you to copy these and assist you with a collection of a particular trade's tools. The local press and local radio may be interested in running a feature which should stimulate local interest. The main library will often have a local history department which may contain a collection of photographs and documents. Back issues of local newspapers could also be helpful in building up a picture of the times and showing which topics might be worth pursuing. The library will also have addresses of local history societies who may be able to help in the gathering of material and making useful contacts. Adult Education Institutes or local Workers Educational Association groups may have tutors available to help develop a project or provide classes to tie in with the project. 'Outreach' classes can be arranged to take place in homes or day centres.

Once the nature of the project is explained, local photographic societies may be able to offer their skills and resources. The copying of old photographs – either as slides or as prints – enables you to hand back photographs that are particularly dear to people or which may not be removed from a collection for fear of being damaged.

Local art or technical colleges may wish to be involved and would be able to help out with printing, developing, mounting and with the more sophisticated skills and equipment needed in the compiling and editing of a tape.

Schools, both primary and secondary, may also be interested in taking part whether on a purely social basis or as a part of a humanities, art or science project.

In addition to all these local sources there are specialist libraries and archives which may also prove helpful. Addresses are on page 47. Some museums and libraries also publish old photographs as postcards – sets of which may be purchased quite cheaply. There are also countless books of old photographs produced by large publishers and small local groups. Some are listed on page 47.

There are also objects and products which are still being made now much as they were years ago – such as blue bag, Sunlight washing soap, glass marbles etc. which in the absence of anything else can also serve as good triggers to memory.

Once you have assembled a variety of objects and photographs you may like to organise it around themes such as Childhood, Outings, Housework, Employment, War etc. Discussion can develop into re-enacting half forgotten activities, games and pastimes. Multi-ethnic groups can produce an even wider range of mementos and compare and contrast memories and experiences.

There are some themes which involve a whole spectrum of ages. Sweet Sixteen[1] is one example. Everybody, old and young contributes something – songs, clothes, photos, mementos etc. which reminds them of when they were sixteen. A party or entertainment on the theme could make a grand climax to the project.

Reminiscence theatre

Reminiscence-based theatre productions have been pioneered over a two-year period by the Exeter based Medium Fare Theatre Company which put together shows and toured the district's hospitals and day centres. This company was encouraged by the ideas developed by the first Reminiscence Aids team. The theatre group gathered material for the shows in a similar fashion to that described above, talking to old people, looking at photographs and objects and noting interesting songs, rhymes and anecdotes. These they employed in short sketches and routines, often in front of the people who had supplied the material. The audience was encouraged to participate and become involved in the show.

Hospital radio

Many large hospitals now have their own radio station. A programme could be based around the reminiscence of some of the patients and staff and integrated with record requests.

It must be obvious from the ideas listed above that the scope for developing *Recall* is almost limitless. In any community there are people with time and skills who would be happy to put them to a new use. The development of *Recall* offers a focus for unusual combinations of talents and people and the opportunity to break away from the labels which beset us such as 'staff', 'clients', 'volunteers', 'professionals', 'teachers', 'pupils', 'young' and 'old'.

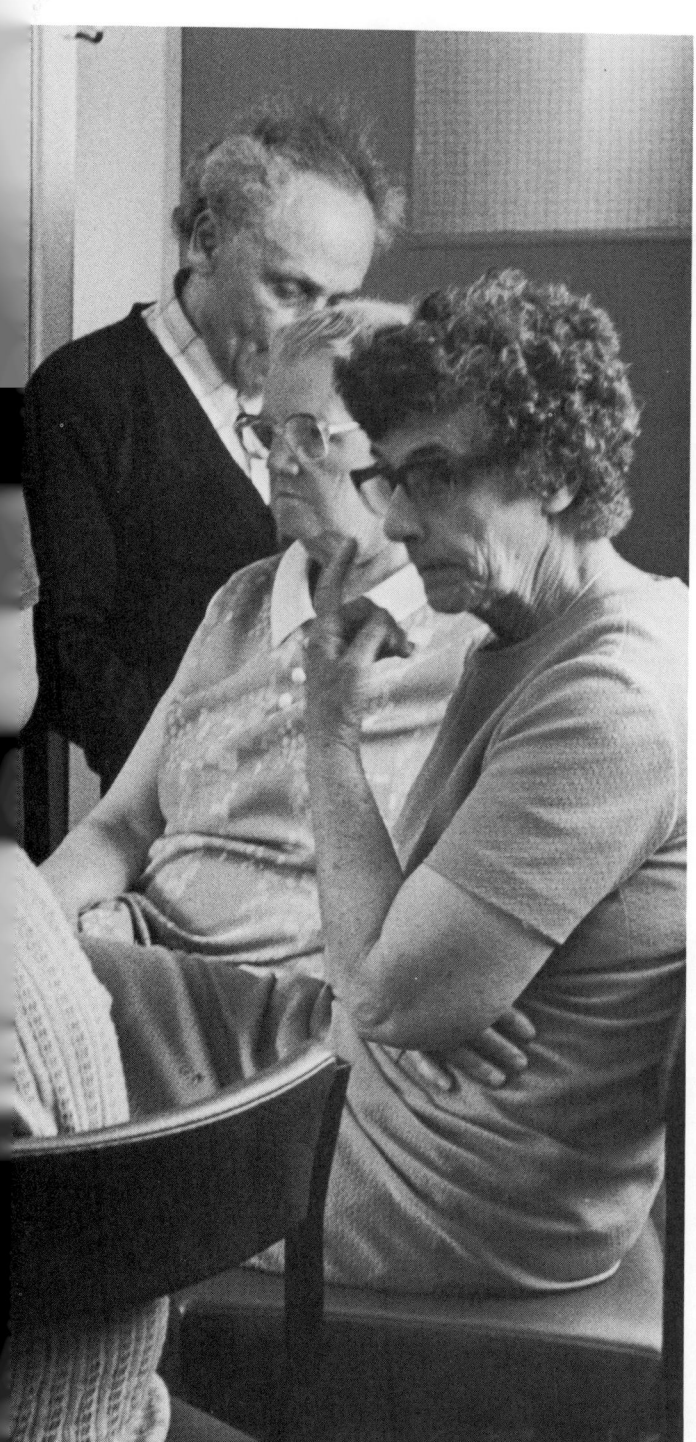

The Sequences

I will stop now. My mind has not dried up but my pen soon will. Hoping these remembrances will have been at least some little help to your project.

As part of the initial research for *Recall* a series of programmes on the radio and a short article in a Sunday paper appealed for memories of the 1920's and 1930's. About 200 replies, some stretching to four or five pages, were received and it was by cross-referencing these detailed memories, related with enthusiasm and humour, that the researchers learnt both what people of the older generations cared to remember and which aural and visual images triggered off these memories.

Despite cultural, class and geographical differences among the correspondents many historically significant – and historically 'insignificant' – events of the last eighty years are remembered with common emotions. Memories relating to childhood predominate, closely followed by reminiscences of the two world wars.

Memories of street life – traders and games, transport, shopping, entertainment, religious and social events and royalty are there, along with brand names of familiar household products, sounds, smells and songs which reawaken old emotions. There are detailed accounts of household expenditure and childhood pocket money – the price of muffins, a dining-room suite, a comic. Memories of childhood friends, enemies, treasured possessions – a large marble, a blue sash, are savoured . . . .

I have so much enjoyed writing this and delving back into the past.

In the following pages, extracts from the many letters received illuminate the introduction to each of the sequences. They evoke a picture of a vanished age. Yet the present is rooted in the past and the people who can remember a different world do us a great service by recalling it for us. They provide a touchstone against which to test the progress of our times.

Childhood

School

Some children with rich parents had lessons at home or went to private schools, but the majority went to the free schools provided by local councils, churches or charity. Discipline was strict and children were encouraged to be clean, obedient and quiet; the cane was used a lot.

I liked my school lessons, but the teachers were so strict that you were afraid to do anything wrong.

Every school day started with lessons in the Christian religion – hymn singing, prayers and bible reading; then there were classes in reading, writing, arithmetic and, for the older children, history and geography. Other lessons included nature study and music (singing songs); there was cookery, needlework and laundry for the girls and gardening and woodwork for the boys. The schools were simple and plainly furnished – very often two or three classes would be going on in one large room.

In the country, children often had to walk two or three miles to school whatever the weather; there was no central heating in schools and those who got wet in the morning had to sit in their wet clothes all day. Many children suffered constantly with coughs and colds. Infectious diseases such as measles, chickenpox and diphtheria were common, sometimes whole schools would be closed down for a time when a lot of children were ill.

There was no secondary schooling except for those who could pay or who were able to gain scholarships. The school leaving age was 14 but children could leave at 12 or even 11 for certain types of work, such as farm work. The type of job a child went to after school depended on the area – whether it was a port, an engineering district, a local mining district etc. There was more choice for boys than girls.

After school I was put to dressmaking, there wasn't much else for girls to do, only going into service or serving in shops.

Every community had its Sunday Schools attached to the church or chapel, to which most children went on Sunday afternoons. Even poor families tried to provide their children with special Sunday clothes, or if not, with their weekday clothes washed on Saturday and ironed and fresh for Sunday. The great day of the year for many children was the Sunday School outing when they would all go to the seaside or the country, if it was not too far away, or for a picnic in a city park.

Streets

There was very little motor traffic before the First World War and the city streets and country roads were much safer than they are now. The streets were lively with human activity: men walked to work in groups or gathered on street corners; women chatted on doorsteps and went to and fro to the shops, to the pawnbrokers or to visit neighbours; street sellers and errand boys carried milk, bread, fish and other goods from house to house.

Those were the days of the muffin man and Hokey Pokey man who carried their wares in a wooden box on their heads. The muffin man used to call '3 a penny muffins – all fresh this morning'. The Hokey Pokey man, 'Hokey Pokey penny a lump', (which was a delicious block of ice cream). To which we would reply – 'The more you eat the more you jump.'

Among all this children ran up and down, playing their games such as leapfrog and 'tip and run' or ball games, hopscotch, skipping and other favourites. Many games had special songs and rhymes to go with them.

Throughout the year children played various games, a great favourite being whip and top. Tops came in various shapes and sizes including spinning jennies and jampots. A great deal of time was spent making patterns on them before spinning them.

Older children often had smaller ones in their care; they would also be called on to run errands for parents or neighbours or to go indoors to help mother – especially the girls! The streets were also places of public entertainment – crowds gathered to watch fights, to listen to the barrel organ, to the preacher or politician and to see the occasional procession or Salvation Army band. In the country there was always something to see out of doors – animals being moved, the blacksmith shoeing horses, wagon-loads of hay or corn coming in from the fields.

Home

When the weather was very bad, children had to find shelter out of doors or stay in their homes. There was hardly any council housing in those days, and there were not enough cheap family sized houses available for everyone to rent. As a result there was much overcrowding. The poorest families in the cities had to live in just one or two rooms but many working-class families managed to get a little house, or half of one, by the time they had several children. It was unusual to have more than two bedrooms and sleeping three or four to a bed was common and at least it was warm!

Electricity was only just becoming available; houses were lit either by gas, oil lamps or candles. There were no labour-saving tools such as hoovers or washing machines and mothers had to work all day long if they wanted to keep the house clean, the children tidy and the meals ready on time. Washday was particularly hard, especially if it rained and the washing had to be dried indoors in front of the coal

fire. The coal fire also had to be used to heat the water for baths and this was often done on Friday or Saturday night.

Bathtime . . . on a Friday night, when we had to get water from an earthenware sink and heat it on a boiler over the hole in the kitchen range, then tip it into the galvanised bath and take it in turns for a dip. Usually myself, female, youngest and cleanest first, then my two brothers and after syrup of figs, whether you wanted it or not, and straight to bed, whatever the time.

Large families of six or seven children and even more were quite common – there was no such thing as Family Planning Clinics then. As soon as the children were old enough they started to help and even contributed small earnings to the family budget. After the rent had been paid the main expense was food – there were no 'convenience' packaged or frozen foods and meals were simple and cheap.

This was also the period up to the First World War when you could buy complete meals for 6 old pennies – meat fourpence, veg one penny, potatoes and pearl barley for another penny. When bread was a penny ha'penny for a loaf and you received a scone for make-weight – for nothing. When my dad managed to get tight for tenpence old money, when fish was ha'penny a piece and chips to go with it a ha'penny – for twopence you could get a feast.

But wages were low too – the agricultural labourers earned as little as twelve shillings a week in some parts and though town wages were higher so were rents. In working-class homes there was constant anxiety about money – not only whether it would last the week but even whether there would be any or not. Many men had irregular work and there was no social security to help the families of the unemployed.

The children of rich parents had a more comfortable life at home, though perhaps they had less freedom to run about. At the other end of the scale there were children who had no parents, left to live in the streets or grow up in institutions.

Slide sequence	Cue questions
1 Childhood.	
2 Morning prayers. The school day began with an assembly of the school for hymns, prayers and notices. As today, the school hall frequently doubled as a gymnasium with wall-bars and other equipment.	*Do you remember going to school? Did you enjoy it? How did you get there? Did you have a morning assembly at school? What happened then?*
3 School photograph. School photographs like this one were taken once a year in the school yard and many old people still treasure their copies; the teacher is wearing a dress in the very plain Edwardian style, buttoned right up to the chin.	*Did you have a school photograph taken? Do you still have any photographs of your school days? Did you have dinner at school or go home at lunch time?*
4 Science lesson. This class of boys is watching two pupils carrying out a simple scientific experiment. There is a diagram on the blackboard. The master's desk is equipped with sink and Bunsen burner.	*Were your teachers strict? Did they use the cane? Were the children well-behaved? What did you call your teachers?*
5 Group photograph. This photograph shows the boys' outdoor clothes of coat, cap and muffler; the long pinafores of the girls show up clearly. The man at the side is well-dressed – perhaps a Sunday School teacher.	*What kind of clothes did you wear to school? Did you have a uniform? What did you wear on Sundays? Did you go to Sunday School? Did you go on Sunday School outings? Did you ever win a Sunday School prize?*
6 School exercise book. The lesson copied out in careful handwriting is about feeding a family. Tea and bread and butter was the usual meal at tea-time in poor homes; watercress was a favourite addition, it was cheap and nourishing. Many mothers made jam at home.	*Have you kept any of your old school exercise books? What lessons did you enjoy?*
7 Classroom. A typical classroom of the period; there are gas lights, framed pictures on the walls and examples of the children's work. The girls wear white pinafores to protect their dresses, and the boys have a type of sailor suit.	*Were there a lot of children in your class? Did the big children teach the little ones? How old were you when you left school?*
8 'Tuppence-coloured'. A comic printed in colour cost as much as most children would have for pocket money in a fortnight. It would be looked after and shared amongst family and friends.	*Did you read comics? Which was your favourite? Did you have pocket money? What did you buy with it?*
9 'Penny-plain'. Cheaper, black and white comics with cartoon strips. This copy of *Butterfly*, advertising 'Film Fun', probably dates from the 1920's when the cinema was becoming popular.	*Did the barrel-organ come down your street? Can you remember any of the tunes it played? Did people like to listen to the music?*
10 Playing in the street. A children's game has been chalked in the cobbled road in the foreground; the girl in the light dress in the centre appears to be skipping and others further down may be playing ball. There appear to be shops at the cross roads in the distance.	*Did you play in the street? Were you allowed to go far from your home to play? Was there much traffic?*

11 Cigarette cards.
Children and young adults loved to collect whole sets of the cards given away in packets of cigarettes. The cards were valuable for learning about many different things as well as giving hours of pleasure in arranging, comparing and exchanging them.

Did you have a collection of cigarette cards? Do you still have it? Which ones did you collect? Can you remember the games you played with them? Did you collect anything else?

12 Leap-frog.
The clogs suggest that this might be a northern scene. Cloth caps were worn out of doors, even when it was warm enough for shirt sleeves.

What games did you play with your friends? Did you play different games at different times of the year? Did you have a hoop? Did you play conkers?

13 Cleaning the streets.
Horse traffic made the streets dirty and, in the hot weather, rather smelly. Here, the water cart from Poplar, East London, is spraying the streets and the boys are cooling their feet behind it. 'Caution – Poison' on the side of the cart probably means that there was disinfectant in the water and it was not for drinking.

What street traders came down your street? Was there a lamplighter?

14 Street scene.
Adults peer into a cart or pram and a group of children pause in their play to watch. The little child on the pavement is wearing an over-large pair of trousers, probably handed down from an older brother. There is quite a lot of traffic at the cross roads at the end of the street.

What singing games did you play? Who looked after the little ones while you were playing?

15 Marbles.
Marbles were a very popular game with both boys and girls; large coloured ones were much prized.

Can you remember any skipping rhymes? What games did you play with marbles? Did you or your parents make any of your toys? Did you play with a doll? What was its name? What was it made of?

16 Wash-day.
With sleeves rolled up and apron on, this lad is helping his mother on wash-day by turning the mangle to squeeze water out of the clothes. Washing is hanging on the line behind him.

Who did the household chores? What were the worst chores? Who did the shopping in your family? What happened on wash day? Did you have a copper? Did you help with the washing or ironing?

17 The family hearth.
The fireplace was the centre of the home and even in very poor families, it was decorated like this one with coloured hangings and ornaments and a bright steel fender. The little gas ring beside the fire could be used to cook on. The table was covered with oilcloth.

Were you ever ill when you were a child? Did the doctor visit the house? Do you remember any of the home remedies for illnesses?

18 Bath-night.
Two other children are waiting in line behind this little girl to have their turn in the tub. There is not a great deal of water to be seen because every drop had to be heated and carried to the bath.

Which night was bath night? How did you heat the water?

19 Tea-time.
This is quite a well-off home – there are books behind father's chair, a table cloth on the table and plenty of food. The children – six of them – seem quite close together in age. The big fireplace, the pictures, wall-paper and the china on the table, all suggest a steady income.

What kind of furniture did you have? Do you remember any of the pictures in your house? What did you have to eat at tea-time?

20 Bed-time.
Three in a bed was quite common in working-class homes; the white sheets and pillow cases are a reminder of how much washing there was to do for a large family. The sturdy iron bed with brass knobs was typical of the period – but in the poorest families children slept on the floor.

Did you have to go to bed at a certain time? How many were there in your family? Did you share a room with any other members of your family? Did you help put the little ones to bed?

The Great War

War was declared against Germany on August 4th 1914. The outbreak of war was not unexpected. During the previous ten years there had been increased spending on armaments and campaigns in the press which had encouraged feelings of national pride and fears of foreign aggression. Much of this propaganda had been aimed quite clearly at Germany.

Thousands of young men rushed to join in with what they thought would be an exciting military adventure. Many of the women who had been campaigning for the vote pledged themselves to support the national struggle against the enemy.

My earliest recollections must be from the First World War, hearing a military band and everyone would run to the front door to watch the soldiers marching down the street and young men and boys falling in behind. I think it must have been a recruiting drive, the volunteers just marched along with them.

Disenchantment was to follow. Life at the Front, in the trenches, was a terrifying and destructive experience. At home, prices rose, some foods like margarine, sugar and meat were in short supply and long hours at work producing goods for the war effort were exhausting many workers.

1914-18 father called up. Shortage of food, especially butter and margarine and having lard in place of butter.

Older people's memories of the First World War tend to reflect these two aspects; excitement and feelings of national pride on the one hand and war weariness and blighted hopes on the other.

I can remember the lovely song 'God Send you Back to Me', which will always stick in my mind. I could sing it right through even now, although I can honestly say I have not heard it since the First World War.

Those elderly people who were young children during the war may remember the ways in which family life changed. With older brothers and fathers away from home in the army or navy there would be fewer wages coming in. At the same time prices were rising rapidly. They may remember having to go without new clothes and making food go further in different ways. From 1917, food shortages meant that many children spent hours in queues outside shops after school and at weekends. Food rationing was introduced in 1918 but unlike the Second World War when this had the effect of spreading supplies equally, many poor people found that they could not afford to buy their share of meat and so did not benefit from rationing.

There were changes in family life for children whose mothers were at work full time in munitions factories. With many fathers away from home, people may remember the ways in which their mothers, aunts and grandmothers took charge of family matters.

For young women it was a time when greater freedom and independence became possible. Those who are old enough to have been at work during the war will probably remember long hours but higher earnings. Opportunities for promotion and more skilled work were possible but for most women it was a question of routine and highly disciplined employment. Some women may remember struggles to keep the family fed and happy during the war. Others may remember the excitement and changes brought about by the war, travelling to visit soldier or sailor relatives and friends, working in strange towns, going to the local cinema and courting.

For men, memories may be about the army and navy or working life. Those who were old enough, fit and whose work was not considered essential will have stories to tell about military life in barracks, camps and at the battle front. For some men the war may be recalled as a time of excitement and glory but many were shocked by their experiences. Some may be eager to describe what happened while

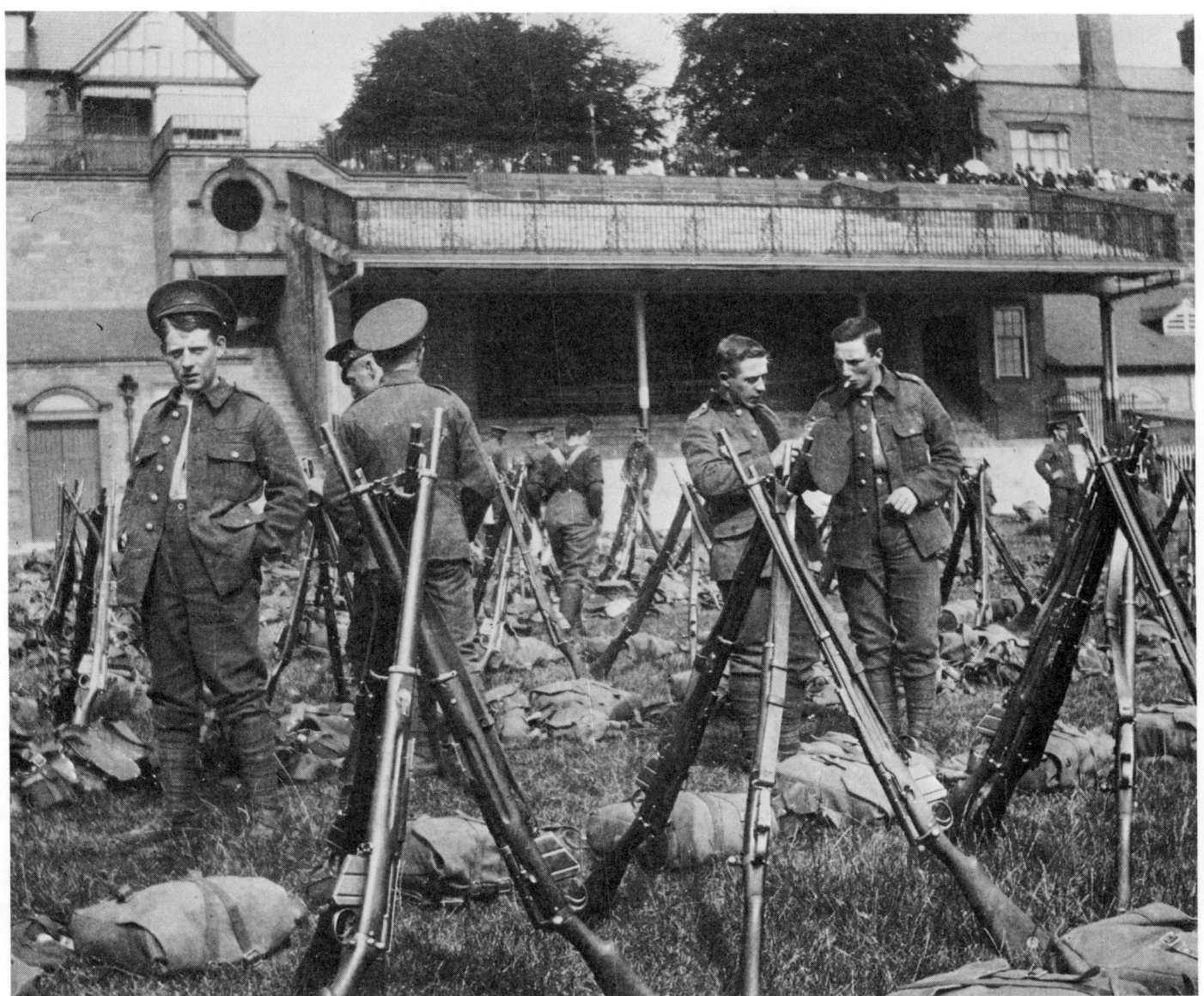

others may still find this difficult over sixty years later. There were of course the conscientious objectors, men whose anti-war principles meant that they were not willing to fight. For them, war memories may be memories of humiliating experiences in prison and in public.

At the end of the war there were mixed emotions. Though immediately people felt relief and the streets filled with noisy, joyful celebrators, there was regret for the thousands of young men who would not return, the thousands more whose lives were wrecked by injuries and a feeling of unease about the future.

On the eleventh hour of the eleventh day of the eleventh month in 1918 we knew the war was over . . . We had a terrific bonfire in the street and my father called out in a loud voice to throw out all your old furniture. After all the drink etc., I think a lot of good chairs and sofas were burnt and the road also caught fire.

I had just met my boyfriend when the 1914 war begun. The 4 years seemed endless. I am not likely to forget 11 November 1918, I was ill in bed with Asian flu which was very prevalent at that time. I could not understand why the

church bells were ringing that Monday morning. My mother came running upstairs crying 'It's peace, it's peace' and I cried too, for joy.

Historians tend to argue about whether the First World War caused a fundamental upheaval in British society or whether the changes which followed were inevitable before 1914. For the generation who have memories of these years the war does seem like a turning point in their own and their families' lives. Few people were unaffected by the war personally and most were to witness changes which tended to make life after the war seem very different to the years before 1914. At the first general election to be held in peace time a slogan was 'Homes Fit for Heroes'. Women over 30 had the vote for the first time ever and a new party, the Labour Party, presented its manifesto to the country. The sacrifices and hard work which people experienced during the war years led them, with the dawning of peace, to expect higher living standards, a fairer deal for women and a political party which would reflect more closely the interests of working people.

Slide sequence	Cue questions

1 The Great War

2 Your country needs you.
In this poster the finger of Lord Kitchener seemed to point directly at each young man in 1914 and proved effective in swelling the ranks of the army before compulsory service was brought in eighteen months later.

How old were you when the war started? Had you left school? Where did you live? What job were you doing if you had started work? What was your father's job then?

3 Queuing to join up.
In the early weeks of the war, thousands and thousands of young men flocked to join the army. Many boys lied about their age, eager not to be left out of what they believed would be a glorious adventure which would be over by Christmas 1914.

Can you remember members of your family or neighbours enlisting? Do you remember boys who lied about their age in order to join up? What happened? Were there any special events where you lived to attract recruits – illuminated tramcars, public meetings?

4 New recruits waiting for the off on a football pitch.
The army made use of parks and open spaces to assemble and drill battalions before leaving by train for the front.

Did you join up at the beginning of the war? Which regiment? Did you join with friends? Can you remember the men in your family going away? Did this make a difference to the family budget?

5 A drink for the soldier.
Differences between a soldier's uniform in 1914 and today include the long jacket, or tunic, breeches and leg wrappings, or puttees as they were known.

What did the soldiers look like in their uniforms? What was in their kit? Can you remember the soldiers in uniform in the streets?

6 Marching soldiers.
During the first few months of the war there were so many recruits that new training grounds had to be opened all over the country and many soldiers had to train with wooden sticks instead of rifles.

Where did the soldiers you knew go to train? Did you visit them? What stories did they tell about life in the army: what was the food like, the long marches and camp life?

7 A postcard from a soldier to his family or loved one.
Most messages from the front were deliberately vague. Army censorship prevented detailed descriptions being sent home and, as conditions at the front worsened, many men were anxious about upsetting families and friends.

Can you remember hearing from soldiers in your family at the Front? Did you write home often from the Front? Do you remember seeing any special decorated postcards for writing to soldiers or for sending back home?

8 Life in the trenches.
Conditions varied but were mostly unpleasant. Apart from the strain of being under fire, there was water, thick mud, lice and the distinctive smell of rotting corpses. All very different from the glorious adventure anticipated by the first volunteers.

What stories do you remember of life at the Front? Were there members of your family injured or killed in battle? Did you know any women who went off to nurse or work with the army?

9 Women loading and lifting sacks of coke.
With 2½ million men under arms, women were called on to do jobs which they had not previously been thought able to do. The readiness of women to work long hours in a wide variety of occupations was to help them win the right to vote after the end of the war.

What work do you remember women doing in the First World War? In your family was there a sister, aunt or your mother perhaps who took up some kind of war work? What was the work: munitions, clothing, engineering, driving?

10 Eat less bread.
Before the war most of Britain's wheat was imported. With these supplies at risk from the action of the German Navy, prices rose rapidly. The government's answer was to fix bread at a lower price, increase the quantity of cheap and coarser flour and encourage people to eat less bread.

People often had to make do with what they had or could get when food was short – do you remember any special recipes which were cooked in your family, e.g., making pastry with fat from a marrow bone?

11 Ration cards and coupons.
By the end of 1917 many foods were in short supply and families were dividing their time between work and queuing outside shops rumoured to be selling margarine, meat, sugar and other foods. By late 1918 sugar, meat, tea and butter were being rationed.

Can you remember queuing for food? What food did people find hard to get? Who did the queuing in your family?

12 The first women tram conductors.
To begin with there was some opposition from men: drivers, conductors and passengers, but eventually as equal wages were established women came to be accepted. Many of these new conductors had been domestic servants before the war and enjoyed the relative freedom, independence and better wages which their new jobs brought them.

Do you remember the first women tram conductors in your town? Were there any other women you remember in unusual jobs? Apart from the long hours of work and overtime were there any other changes for women because of the war? What sort of entertainments do you remember: cinema, get-togethers, outings?

13 Sorting and packing blankets for the troops.
As the war progressed more and more women came into factories and workshops to take the place of men.

Where did people in your family work in the First World War? Do you remember people having exemption certificates and keeping their jobs through the war?

14 Women munitions workers sorting fuses for explosives.
Thousands of women became munitions workers during the war. The work often meant handling dangerous and harmful chemicals and working long hours. The supervisor, a man in overalls and white collar, is standing in the background.

Who were the 'canary girls'? Some women came from other districts to work in munitions – do you remember girls from outside? Where did they live? What was it like working in a munitions factory? Was it very strict? What were the rules? What happened when the men came back from their jobs? Were the women out of work?

15 Air raid precautions.
Though never as severe as in the Second World War, air raids occurred throughout the war. There was no official provision of shelters, except in Dover, where people were accommodated in dug-outs and caves.

Were there any warnings about air raids where you lived? Do you remember the streets being dark at night – without lights? At school, do you remember any special events to do with the war? Did your head teacher tell you about the battles and the victories? Did you have a visit from soldiers or sailors in uniform?

16 A Zeppelin.
These armoured airships flew at low levels and were a terrifying sight to those on the ground. Raids began in mid 1915 and mainly affected London and the south-east.

Did you see a Zeppelin? Did you meet anyone who had seen one? What was it like? What did people feel when they saw one?

17 Destruction caused by a Zeppelin raid.
Zeppelins usually dropped small incendiary bombs which caused damage to property and led to nearly 5,500 people being killed or injured.

Were there any raids in your district? Was there any damage like this (picture)? Did your cinema show any pictures or news about local people in the war?

18 Dancing in the streets on Armistice Day.
As soon as the end of the war was announced in 1918 people ran out into the streets, stopped work and generally enjoyed the sense of relief.

Can you remember hearing the war had ended? What were you doing at that moment? Who told you and how did you feel?

19 Decorated streets celebrating peace.
After the declaration of the Armistice there were days of mixed feelings, high excitement, regrets for the wasted lost lives of young men, hopes for the future but a hatred for the enemy which some politicians were only to eager to encourage as the country began to tackle the problems which four years of war had produced.

Were there celebrations for the end of the war in your street or town? What sort of things happened? Did the men come home straight away or did it take a while before they all came back? Were there many in your family who didn't come back?

20 King George V and Queen Mary.
Through visits to the front and factories during the war the King and Queen had come to be regarded with popular affection. Nevertheless the war had brought changes in British society and the King would have to preside over some difficult times in the coming years including anger and weariness in the Twenties when high levels of unemployment and rising prices made the sacrifices of the war seem to have been in vain.

How do you think people felt at the end of the war? Were they hoping for some changes? Were they just wanting a quiet life? If you think about you and your family before and after the war, were there any changes – for the better or for worse? Did it give you more chances – or did the war mean you were worse off?

Youth

The radio (or wireless, as it was first known) became a popular form of home entertainment in the 1920's; the first sets, which could be made up from cheap do-it-yourself kits, had to be used with earphones or a trumpet loudspeaker. The British Broadcasting Corporation (BBC) was set up in 1926. There were programmes of classical and popular music, talks and readings by well-known people, children's features presented by 'aunties' and 'uncles' and regular news bulletins. These were only broadcast in the evenings, in order not to compete with the sales of daily newspapers. Another form of home entertainment which was becoming more widely available was the gramophone; the first records were not flat, but cylindrical, and played with a scratchy sound.

We had a gramophone, 'His Master's Voice'; you had to wind it up with a handle but it was the latest style, and we had some lovely records.

The dance music played on the radio and on records could also be heard live in concert halls and dance halls, which were especially popular with the young. Old favourites like the waltz and the fox-trot were still popular and the more daring youth tried out the new leg-kicking Charleston. An important new musical influence was jazz, which had crossed the Atlantic from America just before the war. Music was played, too, in the cinemas, to accompany the silent films.

Across the road was a cinema called the Select, but called by us the fleahole. Every Saturday afternoon we would enter this dark smelly fleapit with our four pennies in our hands, threepence for the pictures and a penny for a bar of chocolate. We saw silent films of Charlie Chaplin and Jackie Coogan, Pearl White serials and Tom Mix cowboy epics.

The first 'talkies' with synchronised sound tracks came in 1928. The music halls, with their romantic songs and slapstick comedy, declined in the 1920's in the face of all these new forms of entertainment.

After the First World War there seemed to be a new distance between adults, who had experienced the tragic horror of war, and youth, who wanted to have a good time. This 'generation gap' was noticeable in the dress and behaviour of young women, which often shocked older people. It was fashionable to have short hair and to wear short straight dresses with silk stockings and a minimum of light underwear; this seemed outrageous after the heavy clumsy clothing of the pre-war period but it was certainly healthier and more comfortable. Women did not wear trousers, and it was considered immoral to wear make-up and smoke cigarettes.

There were more jobs for women in the 1920's, though they did not continue to do the heavy work which they had taken over from men during the war. Factories making fabrics, clothes, electrical goods and foodstuffs, and the service industries – transport, communications and offices, provided work for working class girls and the number of women doing domestic service began to decline. Many middle-class girls, who would not even have been allowed to work before the war, found employment in teaching, nursing and the civil service, though in these jobs they had to stop work on marriage.

Boys served long apprenticeships in the skilled trades, or took labouring work or office jobs, but for older men, employment was far from secure. After a temporary economic boom immediately after the war, many industries were struggling in the 1920's and in some parts of the country unemployment was high throughout the decade. Wages were very low for many workers and working conditions were poor – old factories and workshops, for instance, did not have canteens or toilets; rest-breaks and paid holidays were unheard of. Through the unions, which were growing stronger, workers in some industries tried to get better wages and employment contracts. The most famous strike of the time was the General Strike in 1926, when all major industries and transport systems closed down in support of the miners. After nine days normal work was resumed but the experience left many bitter memories, especially among the miners who stayed on strike for another six months.

There was very little help for the poor in the 1920's. War pensions were small, unemployment and sickness pay were limited to certain industries and only lasted a short time; the old, the chronically sick, the disabled and the long-term unemployed all suffered extreme poverty. The only form of Social Security was relief from 'the parish' (the local Board of Guardians). Sometimes this meant being put into the workhouse, an institution which was like a prison and almost as shameful.

Young people usually met their sweethearts locally – in many communities there was a recognised spot for walking about on a Saturday night, when boys and girls would eye each other up and down. Parents were still strict with their daughters, ordering them to be in by nine o'clock at night. Sexual freedom was limited and newly-weds often knew very little about sex, pregnancy and childbirth. However, contraception was becoming more widely practised. Engagements of two or three years were common and during this time the couple would put aside small savings, the boy for a ring, the girl for a few pieces of furniture.

When you got a steady boyfriend with intentions of marriage the girl bought bedding, tablecloths, teacloths, etc., and everything else she would need. Some saved for years, it was known as the bottom drawer, everything you needed went in weekly.

Weddings were often quiet affairs though occasionally it would be an excuse for a big family get-together. Young married couples, unless they were well off and could rent a small house or flat straight away, set up home in one or two rooms, sometimes with their parents. Building Societies were beginning to develop, but it was still more usual to rent a home than to buy. There was a desperate housing shortage, in spite of some new council house building, and many families still lived in slum conditions, over-crowded and without proper sanitation or lighting.

There were many improvements in travelling in the 1920's, with the tram, the motor car and the motor bus, and the greater use of the railways. The suburbs developed around major cities as more people travelled to work instead of walking. The annual holiday was not very common, but outings, with the Sunday School or some other local club, were very popular. Only the rich had private cars, but many people had bikes; bus services were extended into the countryside and many village people travelled away from home for the first time.

I wonder how many people remember the forerunner to the present coaches, namely, the 'chara'. It was a vehicle with two running boards each side to serve as steps. The seats were arranged in rows, each row was the width of the vehicle and there was a door at the end of each row, making a lot of doors each side. In case of rain, a canvas hood had to be manhandled the whole length of the vehicle and secured to the top of the windscreen frame, which was made of wood. Two straps from each side of the windscreen top to the mudguards, supported the hood. The windscreen was vertical and no windscreen wipers in those days. The sides of the vehicle were open to the elements all the time. The tyres were made of solid rubber and the speed limit was 17 miles per hour.

Slide sequence	Cue questions
1 Youth.	
2 His Master's Voice. This was the name of one of the most popular makes of gramophone. Here the man is using a handle to wind up the machine. The music came out of the large decorated horn.	*Did you have a gramophone in your home? Can you remember any of the songs you used to play? Did you have a piano?*
3 Wireless. This is an early wireless, a crystal set. It was called 'wireless' because sound travelled through the air and not, like the telephone, along wires. There was no loudspeaker, so one person at a time listened through earphones.	*How did a crystal set work? Did you know anyone who made one? Was there a wireless in your home? Did you know any other family who had one? Can you remember any of the early programmes?*
4 The modern woman. The short, loose-fitting dress and small hat are typical of young women's fashions in the 1920's; older women usually kept to the pre-war styles, but gradually everyone's skirts crept up to mid-calf. These girls are not wearing gloves which would be considered rather unladylike.	*Can you remember how girls dressed after the First World War? What did your parents think of the new fashions? Did you have your hair cut short? What work did you do? Was it what you wanted to do?*
5 Dole queue. A common sight in areas of high unemployment such as the shipyard towns – men waiting to collect their unemployment pay.	*Were you ever out of work after leaving school? Did you draw the dole? Were your father or brothers ever on the dole?*
6 Bakery. Making bread and other foodstuffs by mass production methods in factories became more common in the 1920's but many traditional small businesses and workshops carried on as before.	*Was there a bakery near your home? Was bread delivered or did you fetch it from a shop? Did you have many tinned or packaged foods to eat?*
7 Cooking the dinner. Many small local bakers provided an extra service to their customers by cooking the Sunday joint and roast potatoes – home ovens were often too small for the job. The young man in the picture looks dressed up for Sunday in a clean shirt and with smartly brushed hair.	*Did you have a special Sunday dinner? Did you have meat on any other day? What did you do after Sunday dinner? Did you have special clothes for Sundays? Did your family go to chapel or church?*
8 Down the back lane. Finding space for drying the washing was hard in the cities before the age of tumble driers. The back lane between the houses was useful for this although it was also a thoroughfare for street traders.	*Which day was wash day? How long did it take to do the wash? How did you get the washing dry in wet weather? What kind of soap did you use?*
9 In the streets. The roads in cities were already crowded with traffic and there were no traffic lights, speed limits or zebra crossings. Trams were a special hazard with steel tracks which could catch a bicycle wheel. Notice the pub sign on the left and the *News of the World* advertisement on the right.	*Did you ever travel on a tram? Did you have a bicycle? Did you know anyone who had a motor car? Which newspaper did your family buy? Who read it? Did you belong to a library?*
10 Blacksmith. As long as there was horse traffic, that is, right up to the Second World War, blacksmiths were needed to fit the horses with fresh shoes. Here he is just hammering a horse shoe into shape. Notice his work plans and measurements chalked up over the fire.	*Was there a blacksmith near where you lived? Did you ever watch the blacksmith at work? Did you ever ride a horse, drive a cart or work with horses? Was the horse traffic dangerous to children?*

11 The General Strike.
The *Daily Express* announces the General Strike. Local and national papers did not come out during the strike. The trade unions and the government each produced their own newspapers.

Do you remember the General Strike? What was it about? How did it affect the place where you lived? Were you on strike? Was your father or mother on strike? Was there any conflict in your family over the strike?

12 Travel to work.
People used private transport to get to work during the strike, as all regular services of public transport were closed down. Only essential foodstuff was moved, sometimes by soldiers.

Did you go to any meetings or demonstrations during the strike? Did you see any buses being driven by students? Was there a food shortage?

13 Queuing up.
These young women are probably queuing for the cinema, a concert or the dance hall. Notice how they are all dressed in much the same style.

Did you go out much with other young people? What sort of dances were popular?

14 Pawn shop.
The sign of the pawn shop was three golden balls hanging over the shop door. Clothes and other household items could be exchanged for cash; this was usually done at the beginning of the week. On pay day the goods were bought out again. It was a sort of poor woman's credit bank.

Was there a pawn shop near where you lived? Did your mother put things in to pawn? Do you know how much housekeeping money your mother had? Could she buy things on credit at the local shops?

15 The Salvation Army.
The Salvation (or 'Sally') Army was one of many charitable institutions which provided food and lodging for the homeless poor; they also gave help to poor people in their own homes. Salvation Army bands provided free street entertainment too.

When times were hard where did people go for help? What kind of assistance did the Salvation Army give? Was there a Salvation Army citadel near your home?

16 Fish and chips.
This was already a popular food, along with hot pies and other things which could be bought to eat in the street.

Could you buy any ready cooked food in the shops? Did any vans come round selling hot food? Did you often have fish and chips?

17 Silent films.
The early 1920's was the great age of silent comedy and adventure films, often shown in serial form. Pearl White was one of the stars usually left in a perilous situation at the end of each episode.

Did you go to the cinema when you were young? How often did you go? Do you remember any films you particularly liked? Who were your favourite film stars? Did your parents go to the pictures? What was different about going to the pictures in those early days?

18 Going to the pictures.
A large queue of people waiting to go into the Empire cinema; the first house seems to be just coming out. Some people are arriving or leaving by taxi.

Was there a cinema near your home? How much did it cost to go in? Did you go with friends? Did you go when you were courting?

19 Music hall.
Marie Lloyd epitomises for many the great age of the music hall. By the 1920's the widespread popularity of the music hall was facing competition from the exciting new 'picture houses'.

Did you ever go to a music hall? Can you remember any of the songs that they used to sing or the acts that were performed?

20 Lyons tea shop.
A private party, perhaps of special guests, arriving at a Lyons tea shop and being greeted by the waitresses. These restaurants by providing good meals at reasonable prices encouraged people to eat out more.

Do you remember the Lyons tea shops? Did you ever eat out? What sort of meals could you have? How much did it cost? Did you go to restaurants very often?

Living through the Thirties

During the 1930's a whole range of new, mass-produced consumer goods became widely available for the first time. Electric household appliances, such as cookers, carpet cleaners, irons and washing machines, made housework easier and reduced the demand for domestic servants. There were cheap family motor cars and other luxury goods such as radios, gramophones, telephones, modern furniture and household fittings and a whole range of items made in the new plastics and rayons. Thousands of private and council houses were built between the wars; with the growth of building societies, this meant that more and more people could live in a family house and even own their own home. Cheap, fast transport encouraged people to move out to the suburbs which were growing round all the major cities. These new estates were the tramping grounds of the door-to-door salesmen who introduced house-wives to new products and encouraged payment by hire purchase – though many people still preferred to pay in full.

You could furnish a house on less than £100. I still have my list of furniture we bought out of £100. I married in 1938. Three piece suite, £13.13s.; dining room suite, £17.17s.; bedroom suite and bed, £17.17s.; Axminster Carpet (3 × 2½ yds), £4.10s. After washing tub, clothes pegs, table top mangle, pots, pans, etc., we still had £20 in the bank and better furniture than you get today.

Not everyone could afford the new living standards; hundreds of thousands still lived in slum conditions, without electricity or bathrooms and with scarcely enough money to feed and clothe themselves. Many people still began married life in one or two rooms and had to save up for any new furniture. However, food prices remained fairly stable and as the economy began to pick up towards the end of the decade, it was possible to see that, overall, living standards had improved.

The 1930's are always associated with high unemployment. This was worst in South Wales, the North East, parts of Scotland and the textile towns of Lancashire and Yorkshire. Britain's traditional industries – textiles, shipbuilding, mining, heavy engineering and manufacturing – were in decline and many men found themselves out of work in early middle age or even earlier, unable to support their families. There was much suffering from cold, hunger, disease and even malnutrition amongst all ages; medical care was scarce and expensive. Unemployment pay and National Assistance money were scarcely enough to live on; by selling what they had, using the pawn shop and keeping a tight budget, people managed for as long as they could before seeking help from the state or from charity.

Any woman worked very hard in those days, everyone used the pawn shop. No Social Security or whatever, they would sell furniture to buy food.

When the Government tried to economise by reducing the rates of National Assistance or by introducing a Means Test, there was fierce opposition. Thousands of unemployed people took part in Hunger Marches from the North and West to London to draw public attention to their desperate plight. Soup kitchens, shelters and social clubs were set up by charities and the workers themselves to help the unemployed and the government established re-training camps – but proper work was the only solution and it was slow to come.

Employment was higher in the South, the East and the Midlands, where new factories were built to produce electrical goods, motor cars, processed foods, artificial fibres, plastic goods and aeroplanes. Office work, transport, the post office and the press were other expanding areas of employment and there were also more shops, hairdressers, garages, laundries and other services.

Altogether the 1930's were a time of great contrasts – the modern factory and the craft workshop, Woolworths and the rag-and-bone man, the suburban semi and the inner-city slum, mass unemployment and the family car, the cries of street sellers and the noise of motor traffic.

You don't hear young men whistling in the street any more, or anybody singing about their work, like street sweepers and window cleaners, and grocer boys and paper boys; muffin sellers on Sundays, and cries of 'ripe strawberries', 'lavender' and the herb lady at Camden Town.

The 1930's were also a time of momentous national events, which made a great impact on the whole population through the national press and radio. The death of George V was soon followed by the sensational abdication of his successor, Edward VIII. He had fallen in love with a divorced American, Mrs. Simpson; as head of the Church of England, the king could not be allowed to marry a divorced person, so he gave up the throne.

When the Duke of Windsor made his abdication speech, we were sitting in the living room waiting, as we had been told that he would speak to the nation over the wireless. After we had heard him we all felt very sad, almost like a family loss.

This was followed by the coronation of a new king and queen – George VI and Queen Elizabeth (now the Queen Mother). This occasion was celebrated by street parties in many areas.

The Civil War in Spain in 1936 and '37 excited a great deal of political controversy and some men went to fight as volunteers in the International Brigades. Hitler's rise to power in Germany, the fear

of another war and the question of re-armament, were all issues which were widely discussed.

As conditions in both the home and the workplace improved, there was also more time and opportunity for leisure. The pubs remained a lively centre of traditional community life.

I remember the Feathers public house, open until 12 o'clock at night, and the men and women getting drunk and fighting or being turned out. My mum had my grandad's police whistle (he was retired) and she used to stand on our roof garden and blow the whistle and the cops came and broke up the fights and nobody knew who blew the whistle.

At home the radio and the gramophone became more popular and there was a growing readership for comics, hobby magazines and paperback books as well as the daily press. About a quarter of the population went to the cinema once a week; many people also went dancing and to concerts and the theatre. Travel – by rail or bus, private car and particularly bikes – was cheap and more accessible to people for both work and pleasure. Family outings were easier – people were keeping their families small as part of the move towards better living conditions. The paid holiday, increasingly common during the decade, became a right just before the Second World War. Seaside resorts, with their boarding houses, amusement arcades and fun fairs, were growing and the first Butlins holiday camp was opened in 1937. Youth hostelling, hiking and

camping holidays were popular with young people. Few people travelled abroad on holiday, though cruises on the great ocean liners, from Liverpool and Southampton, were taken by the rich. City people especially were now better able to fulfill a long-felt need for the freedom and fresh air of the countryside and the sea.

Slide sequence	Cue questions
1 Living through the Thirties.	
2 Living room. Most homes were heated by coal fires and the hearth was the centre of the home. An important part of women's work was making and mending clothes. Notice the low, 'modern' mantlepiece and the radio on the bureau.	*Did you make the children's clothes? Which room did you use most? Can you remember how it was furnished? Did you buy new furniture?*
3 Sale time. Sale time was as popular then as it is now; furnishing and dress material was especially sought after. Every woman is wearing a hat – it was not done to go out bare-headed. The exception is the shop assistant.	*Where did you do most of your shopping? Was there a market near your home? Did you ever buy things in a sale? Did you have many new clothes?*
4 Rinsing the washing. Although washing machines were available, many women still did their weekly wash in the traditional way using a copper and a mangle. This girl is probably helping her mother by rinsing washing under the cold water tap in the scullery.	*What arrangements did you have for washing? Did you ever get a washing machine? Did you have an electric iron? Was it as hard as it had been for your mother?*
5 Listening to the wireless. These two children are enjoying a radio programme on a large expensive set. The BBC kept extending the range and variety of programmes. Children's programmes were very much loved.	*Did you have a wireless? Did your children listen to the children's programmes? Can you remember any of the programmes?*
6 The Prince of Wales and Mrs. Simpson. Prince Edward should have been crowned king following the death of his father, George V. Instead he chose to marry Mrs. Simpson and his brother became King George VI.	*Do you remember hearing the abdication announcement? Did you feel that the Prince of Wales did the right thing? Do you remember the coronation of George VI?*
7 Chimney sweep. He was a regular visitor as so much coal was burnt. Everything had to be covered up to protect it from the soot and there would be a good scrubbing down when he had gone. His white apron is to indicate how clean and efficient he is.	*Did you have coal fires? Did the chimney sweep come round? Did this make a lot of extra work? Did you ever have gas or electric fires?*
8 Rag and bone man. As people bought new things for the home they threw out their old wooden and metal possessions to the rag and bone man, usually for nothing, though sometimes he gave a few coppers.	*Do you remember the rag and bone man coming round? Did he give you anything in exchange? Do you think he made a living from it?*
9 Coal cart and the inspector. The coal man was a regular caller at every house. Here he is having his bags checked for the correct weight by an official inspector. The coal cart is horse drawn but the inspector has a motor lorry.	*Do you remember the coal man coming round? How much was a bag of coal? How much coal did you need in a week, or a month? Was there ever a shortage of coal?*
10 Flower and vegetable market. This could be a wholesale market like Covent Garden. Usually flowers and vegetables were sold from stalls in the street.	*Did you have a garden or an allotment for growing flowers and vegetables? Did you buy them from a market?*

1 Market stall.
Shops and markets were often kept open until quite late at night; goods were often sold cheaply, especially on Saturday nights. Notice the boys with the bicycle in the background and the brass scales on the stall.

Where did you do your shopping? Did you shop around for bargains very much? Did you shop every day or just at the weekend? Could you get credit in the shops?

2 Men queuing.
These men may be queuing up to draw unemployment pay or national assistance, or even for a food hand-out.

Were you ever out of work in the 1930's? What happened to people who were out of work for a long time? Did this happen to many people?

3 Funeral.
Most people were buried in graves rather than cremated and funerals were splendid though solemn affairs, with black horses and many flowers. Neighbours closed their curtains as the procession went past. Children's funerals, much more common then, were particularly moving.

Do you remember any funerals in your family? Was a funeral very expensive? How did people manage to pay these expenses? Did everyone wear black clothes in mourning?

4 Camberwell Defence March.
Mass meetings and marches were features of the period; as well as the trade unions there were many political organisations such as the Unemployed Workers Movement.

Did you belong to a political organisation or trade union? Did you go to any marches or meetings?

15 The Jarrow Crusade.
Jarrow was a shipyard town in the north-east which suffered very high unemployment in the 1930's. People marched from Jarrow to London to draw attention to their plight.

Do you remember the Jarrow Crusade? Did you see the marchers? Did you know why they were on the march? What was done to help them?

16 Blackshirts.
The Blackshirts (called after their uniform) were an extreme right-wing group who supported the ideas of Hitler in Germany. There were many clashes between fascists and communists in the 1930's. The leader of the Blackshirts was Oswald Mosley.

Do you remember the Blackshirts? Did you know what they stood for? Did you ever see any Blackshirts meeting or holding demonstrations?

17 Milk bar.
An interest in health and the work of the Milk Marketing Board encouraged people to drink more milk, or milk shakes, in the 1930's. Milk bars appeared – perhaps as an alternative to pubs.

Did you buy milk for your children? Did you ever go to a milk bar? Was milk delivered in bottles or from a churn? How much did it cost?

18 Steam train.
Most trains ran on coal fired engines and carried their own supplies of coal. There were four railway companies, and the engines were usually brightly painted. A journey by train was still an adventure for many children.

Did you travel to work on a train? Did you live near a railway station? Do you remember the first electric trains? How much did it cost to travel by train?

19 Ice-cream parlour.
These girls enjoying ice-cream are evidently on holiday at the seaside. Bathing costumes were quite skimpy in the 1930's, though the two-piece was still considered rather daring.

Did you ever go on holiday in the 1930's? Where did you go and how did you get there? Did you stay in a boarding house? Did you ever go Youth Hostelling?

20 At the seaside.
Seaside holidays became more and more popular in the 1930's with cheaper travel and longer paid holidays. The summer of 1939 was overshadowed by the threat of Hitler and the coming war.

Did you ever take your children to the seaside? What were the popular seaside resorts in those days? Did you get paid holidays from work?

The Second World War

The Second World War began for Britain in September 1939; although it was not entirely unexpected, it was still shocking, and many people remember exactly what they were doing when the news was announced.

On the Sunday morning of 3rd September, Neville Chamberlain came on the air. My parents, husband and I were all in the same room, expectant. I clearly remember I was shelling peas for lunch. Gravely the Prime Minister made the statement: 'I have to tell you that a state of war now exists between us and the German Nation.' We were stunned, but mechanically I kept shelling peas. Suddenly my father snapped at me, 'How can you go on shelling peas at such a time?' I snapped back, 'And how do you think we can win the war if everyone downs tools?'

Everyone expected that bombing raids would begin at once; some women and children had already been evacuated from the most threatened areas.

My recollection of the second world war, was my mother-in-law stuffing bags of sand up the chimney in her house the day war was declared and the sirens went for the first time.

In fact there was a period of relative calm at home in the first months, and some of the evacuees came home again. Meanwhile the army was mobilised and young men were called up. There were many sad partings as the troops left for the Continent. Through the radio and other forms of entertainment popular singers like Vera Lynn expressed the national feeling of sorrow, determination and hope.

In these first months of the war, even though Germany had successfully invaded Poland and Scandinavia, there were still hopes of negotiating a peace settlement. However, all such hopes had been abandoned by May 1940, when Germany invaded Holland and Belgium. At the same time Winston Churchill became the new Prime Minister. The German Army advanced rapidly into France and in June the famous Dunkirk operation took place when thousands of French and British soldiers were brought safely across the Channel to England.

With France now under enemy occupation, the British people felt that they stood alone against the might of the enemy. The Home Guard was mobilised as a civilian defence force against the expected invasion of German paratroopers. In fact, the immediate fighting was not so much on the land as in the skies. Bombing raids began in July, but the intense aerial fighting of the Battle of Britain, as it

came to be called, lasted from August 15th to September 15th. It ended in triumph for the British Air Force, and the Germans abandoned their plans for an invasion. Aerial bombing continued throughout the war, causing terrible damage to towns and cities, and many civilian casualties, on both sides.

After this, the arena of the war was gradually extended. Germany invaded the Soviet Union in June 1941; in December of the same year the Japanese air force attacked the American base at Pearl Harbour and the war became truly a world war. Men and women in the British armed forces were drafted to different parts of the world; many of them died in the fighting, others ended up as prisoners or came home wounded and disabled. In Britain, soldiers, sailors and airmen from other countries mingled with the civilian population – the Americans in particular are remembered; there were also refugees from Europe and even German prisoners of war.

The spirit of national unity and the widespread certainty, even in the most desperate moments of the war, that Britain would win in the end, meant that people accepted restrictions on their freedom which would have been unacceptable in peace. Everyone was expected to contribute to the war effort, to 'do their bit'. Able-bodied men were either conscripted into the armed forces or directed into essential work at home – making armaments or working in the mines and railways. As the war demanded more and more fighting men, women, too, were drawn into essential production doing heavy 'men's work' in factories and farms. Married women, even those with children, were expected to work – if only part-time or in the voluntary services. Many people at the end of a day's work went on duty as fire-watchers or air-raid wardens. Refugees, evacuees and essential workers were billeted on any homes with space to spare.

In some places air raids became a regular feature of life, terrifying and destructive but something which people learned to live with. Some made temporary homes in air raid shelters, others would not be persuaded to move and sheltered in their own kitchens. People with gardens often had their own Anderson shelters, others used large communal shelters; in London many people spent their nights on the platforms of the Underground stations.

Living in London during the war and the sirens going regularly as clockwork at six pm, when the docks were being bombed. Spending the nights with the young baby in the cellar, coming up to find windows blown in and furniture pitted with glass; putting up fresh blackout.

The blackout was strictly enforced; every chink of light had to be covered at night and 'Put that light out' became the catch phrase of the war at home.

Outside at night the darkness was complete, making travelling and rescue work difficult.

Another problem was shortages of food, clothing and other necessities. In order to provide enough essentials to go round, the government regulated production, subsidised food, taxed luxury goods and issued ration books.

Clothing and food rationing came into being, eggs seemed to disappear, you were lucky if you got one a week for the whole family. You or one of your family had to queue for fish if the fishmonger had any delivered.

It was hard for large families but people soon managed to combine the hard-to-get ingredients with a degree of inventiveness, to make the food go further.

The ingenuity of the housewives was astonishing. Malt loaves were made from extract of malt, and there were sponge cakes made from liquid paraffin.

Many other equally inventive recipes were devised and often broadcast over the wireless on programmes such as 'The Kitchen Front'.

A 'black market' came into existence, circulating luxury goods, such as nylon stockings and cosmetics, at high prices.

In spite of the preoccupation of the war, and in some ways because of it, there was much talk of social change. With Russia fighting on the side of the Allies there was a great deal of pro-Soviet feeling, easily translated into an enthusiasm for socialist ideas and practices. Apart from this there was a growing determination not to go back to the grim days of the 1930's; these were symbolised for many people in the film 'Love on the Dole', made in 1943 and based on the famous novel by Walter Greenwood. Many reports and proposals about the possibility of greater social equality were published during the war, notably the Beveridge Report. This idealism was to find expression in a resounding victory for the Labour Party in the General Election which followed the end of the war.

The war against Germany ended on May 8th 1945 (V.E. Day), with the unconditional surrender of the German army (although the war against Japan continued for another three months). Joyful celebrations began immediately.

It was a very exciting moment when the lights went on again when the war ended. V.E. and V.J. days were times of fun with dancing at night on the square, streets were decorated and there were endless street parties.

Slide sequence	Cue questions

1 The Second World War

2 War declared.
The Prime Minister, Neville Chamberlain, announced on the radio that Britain was at war with Germany. Most people would have heard the news on the radio but details were given in the papers.

Do you remember war being declared? How did you hear the news? Were you surprised? What were you doing at the time?

3 Soldier's farewell.
Departures such as this must have been a common sight on railway stations and at docks. This soldier's pith helmet suggests he was going to one of the hotter countries and not Europe.

Did you or your husband join the services? Did either of you go overseas? Did you see much of the soldiers in the street?

4 Evacuee children.
Goodbyes already over, these children who are being evacuated from London for safety, as were many, are on their way to stay in private houses in various parts of the country. For most, it was the first time they had left home – or London.

Were you or your children evacuated? What sort of places did the evacuees go to? Did most people come back eventually? Were the evacuation children well cared for?

5 Preparing vegetables in an Anderson shelter.
Although the air raids were disruptive, coming at any time of the night or day, people became accustomed to dropping everything and hurrying to shelter. Many however became sufficiently organised to take whatever they were doing at the time with them.

Was there much bombing near your home? Did you go to a shelter? Did you have a shelter in your home or garden? Where did you shelter if there was an air raid when you were away from home?

6 The sandbagged entrance of an air raid shelter.
Shelters varied – some (such as Anderson shelters) were in the gardens of houses, others were communal in public places. This one seems to be a larger, well-built communal one in a park.

Did you spend many nights in an air raid shelter? What did you take with you into the shelter? Did you ever stay at home during the raids?

7 Bomb damage.
After the raids people surfaced not knowing whether their homes would still be there. Anything still intact was removed from the debris. Even if the house was still standing, if the windows had not been taped, the contents might be pitted with broken glass.

Was there much bomb damage near your home or place of work? Was your own home badly damaged? Did you have to move away because of the bomb damage?

8 Sewing blackout curtains.
Curtains were not the only form of blackout. There were also recipes for blackout dye which was painted on to the windows.

Did you make blackout curtains for your home? How did people find their way about at night in the blackout? Did you ever have to travel during the blackout?

9 ARP Warden.
Men not enlisted took up various jobs on the home front. Wardens were very important, offering not only practical help by enforcing laws but also keeping up morale by their attitudes and indomitable spirits. Many had other jobs during the day.

Do you remember the ARP wardens? What did they do exactly?

10 Utility clothes.
Because of shortages of raw materials and labour, controls were introduced to ensure that the best possible clothing could be supplied at a reasonable price. Utility clothes were made to a government standard and eventually there were rules regulating the number of pleats and pockets and the length of socks.

Do you remember rationing? Did you have clothing coupons? What sort of things were in short supply? Could you buy nylon stockings?

11 Coupon book.
Many things were rationed – food first, clothes later. The coupon system was devised to ensure equal shares and distribution. In some areas, however, there were black markets where extra things could be bought.

Did you have to queue for food? Could you get enough to eat? What sort of food did you have at Christmas time in the war?

12 Winston Churchill with his habitual cigar.
Winston Churchill, as Prime Minister, led the coalition government during the war. People gathered round radios to listen to his powerful and inspiring speeches.

Did you listen to Winston Churchill on the radio? What did people think of him? Did you ever see him?

13 Girls with gas masks listen to a broadcast.
In factory 'pinnies' and uniforms these girls wear the gas masks which ultimately were not needed, although one of the biggest fears at the beginning of the war was of gas attacks. Everyone was obliged to carry a mask and there were special ones for babies and older children.

Do you remember hearing Lord Haw Haw on the radio? Did you have a gas mask? Did you ever think you might be gassed? Did people carry their masks about with them?

14 A young mother listening to the radio in a prefab.
Those people who were bombed out were fairly quickly rehoused in prefabs intended only as temporary accommodation but far outlasting their predicted lifespan.

Do you remember the prefabs? Did you ever live in one? What radio programmes did you enjoy listening to during the war? Do you remember Itma or the Hi Gang Show?

15 Soldiers embarking.
One of the many troop ships leaving for the war front, officers and men are watched by a small group of civilians. Usually a special leave was granted before soldiers went to the front. Sometimes leave was heartbreakingly short – only a few hours.

Did you, your husband or any of your relatives go overseas to fight? Whereabouts did you/he go? Did you lose anyone close to you in the war?

16 Piccadilly Underground station with sleeping people.
The Underground stations were natural shelters during the air raids and many people slept there through the night. Early morning commuters grew to accept the sight of them as they set off to work.

Did you know that people slept in the Underground shelters during the bombing? Did you ever do that?

17 A woman munitions worker.
Many women learnt the factory skills required for munitions production in the absence of all the young men. All available iron and aluminium, including railings and saucepans, was collected and channelled into the war effort.

Did you or any of your family do any factory work? Work in the Land Army? What sort of work did the women do? How did they get on with the men in these jobs?

18 Vera Lynn reading a postcard from 'One of the Boys'.
Vera Lynn became the idol of British forces overseas – her songs expressed the sentiments of those at home and far from home and she herself helped to sustain morale by her many concerts and visits to the armed forces.

Do you remember Vera Lynn? What other singers were there? Do you remember any of the songs that were popular during the war?

19 Crowds in Leicester Square celebrate peace.
As they had pulled together to survive the war so they came together to celebrate. Crowds descended on any public place in hundreds and thousands.

Where were you when the war ended? How did you hear the news? (If abroad) When did you get home? Did you join in any of the victory celebrations? Was there a party in your street?

20 A soldier returns to his family.
Although the war ended in 1945, many soldiers serving abroad did not get home until months or years later. The church bells, which had been silent during the years of the war, rang out for peace.

What sort of changes did the war make in your life? Do you think that things were better generally after the war than before? What do you think was the biggest change brought about by the war?

A Different World

As I went to sleep lulled by the sound of traffic, a loose drain cover would make the sound of 'clunk clink' as the traffic passed over it. To me as a child that was the most comforting and reassuring noise.

The soldier returning to his home from the Second World War, expected to find changes for the better in the world he had fought for. But things did not work out quite as people had hoped.

True, as Vera Lynn had promised, the lights had gone on again and, to his relief, the dole queue seemed to have shrunk, if not vanished altogether, but there were still queues, now for bread, meat, fuel. Luxuries longed for in the jungles of Burma or on the heaving grey waters of the Atlantic were in short supply, if indeed they could be obtained at all.

Post-war Britain was to see some changes in family life. Those women who had developed a taste for independence during the war found that they were expected to confine themselves to looking after home, husband and children. Housebuilding programmes transformed towns and countryside as new towns and large estates spread out. Many people moved to find work or housing: old friendships came to an end and family ties were loosened. During the war, there had been a great dispersal of the population, many people married those whom otherwise they would never have met – sometimes this meant settling down in quite another part of the country.

There were great changes, too, in the lives of older people who came from overseas to work and make a new life. To grow old in a land which is not the land of birth is not unusual but neither is it always an easy experience. Grandchildren who quickly grow up in a culture and way of life which is unfamiliar can seem distant but there will always be opportunities to meet at the temple, church, synagogue or mosque and talk over old times.

The welfare state meant free health care initially, and a more comprehensive social insurance system. The fear that sickness could not be afforded or that a whole family's standard of living might be reduced by the ill health of one member was to be removed.

There were holidays too. Suddenly most wage earners were entitled to a paid holiday and the cost was low enough to mean travel to parts of the world hitherto only imagined. Holiday Camps and resorts all round the coast called for patronage. For almost the first time in history the worker seemed to be in a buyer's market.

The pace of life quickened. Lumbering tramcars that had groaned their way through the streets gave way to the quieter, swifter trolley-buses. Steam trains were replaced by diesels and electric trains . . . not without regrets.

Flying became commonplace and while traffic on the roads was often a source of worry and fear to those who remembered more leisurely times, there was now speedier road transport as the great motorways were carved out.

As the decades passed, family life seemed to turn in on itself. Radio had done its share in keeping people within their own homes, but television ensured it. No longer was it necessary to go out for entertainment: it entered the home, it was there by the fireside.

Young people seemed to be expressing, in more and more ways, their own individuality, rejecting what they saw in adult society. Their messages came through in clothes and music. There was a new questioning of the value of family life which many in the older generation took for granted. The idea that a woman's place was in marriage and in the home was no longer just accepted – nor was it considered just or fair that in work she should earn less than a man at the same job. Within the family this meant changes; marriage was no longer almost universally considered a lifelong arrangement, though it became no less popular amongst the divorced population. Men and women's roles blurred as men took to pushing prams and cooking meals while women took a place as workers in factory and office.

So we are suddenly at the present day . . . a world so different from that fifty years ago that we might wonder if it really is the same place. Even the pattern of such a mundane activity as shopping has changed completely. Only milk and newspapers are regularly delivered at the door where the greengrocer, baker, butcher and grocer all used to call. Now we serve ourselves from the shelves of supermarkets as shop counters disappear and we can buy our food frozen for eating weeks or months ahead.

Refrigerators, washing-machines, television sets, hair-driers, personal calculators – all wildly fantastic imaginings half a century ago – are now looked on as near essentials.

My generation saw the first cars, the first aeroplanes, the first airship, everything right through to the first man walking on the moon; progressed from the earth closet to the modern bathroom and modern kitchen . . . we have seen all modern inventions and technology . . . lived through two wars.

Unbelievable things have been achieved: perhaps there are even greater things to come. To a generation that has seen a flag placed on the moon and the earth surrounded by whirling satellites, nothing would seem impossible.

Slide sequence	Cue questions
1 A Different World.	
2 Shopping queue. Food rationing continued into the 1950's: it was to be quite some time before food supplies approached anything like pre-war levels. Queuing was a wearisome and time consuming chore particularly during the long hard winter of 1947.	*What were your feelings in 1945? What sort of changes did you want to see? What was it like in that hard winter of 1947?*
3 Friends and neighbours. Chatting over the fence means a welcome break from housework. After the war increasing numbers of women were taking on two jobs: caring for a home and family during the day and going out to work in the evening.	*Were you rehoused after the war? Did your family all live quite near? Did anyone emigrate abroad? What kinds of new factories and workplaces were there in your area in the years after the Second World War?*
4 Bobby on the beat. The neighbourhood policeman would be known to everyone in the community. Although children did not always appreciate a firm hand, he was, in general, someone who could be approached for help. The bobby on the beat gave way to impersonal patrolling panda-cars but now, once more, policemen are returning to the beat.	*When you were young was there a local policeman where you lived? Did you know him? If there was trouble what happened?*
5 The new pram. Everyone crowds round to admire the new baby *and,* a rare event in the 1930's, the new pram. After the Second World War a whole new baby-care industry grew up, reflecting greater affluence and a greatly increased interest in the early years of childhood.	*What prams or pushchairs did you have in your family? What happened if anyone had twins? Of all the advantages which today's young parents have, which is the best – disposable nappies, washing machines, playgroups and nurseries, cheap toys?*
6 Playmates. In modern housing schemes the asphalt play spaces replacing streets and pavements of an earlier time may be safer but they have little for the imaginations of children to work on. And today's inner cities offer little space for self-expression and development for young people from richly diverse cultural backgrounds.	*What sort of game would you have played in a space like this? What was your favourite place to play in? Do you remember 'plaguing' or playing tricks on adults when you were young?*
7 At home. Even if three generations did not always live together under one roof the chances were that grandparents were never far away. This old lady seems happy in her surroundings: the range, mantelshelf and dresser all seem to belong to an earlier age. But new housing, welcome though it was, often broke up the old communities and families found the small new houses and flats left little room for the oldest generation.	*Do you remember your grandparents? Where did they live? If someone who was very old fell ill, what would happen?*
8 Full house. To sit for hours in the warm, scented darkness with the sound of the 'mighty Wurlitzer' organ, waiting for that white beam of light to fix on a world of fantasy was an opportunity to escape from harsher realities outside.	*What was your local picture house? Is it still there? Have you been to the cinema recently? What film did you see?*
9 The stars: Errol Flynn and Olivia De Havilland. In the golden age of the cinema the 'stars' were the fashion leaders whose style was copied with devotion and whose private lives were detailed in fan magazines. Today their old fans can relive the passions and excitement – on the smaller screen of their own television sets.	*Do you remember the first talking pictures? If you had the chance what film would you like to see again now?*

Out of work.
Film stars and cinemas provided an escape from the grim and soul destroying realities of unemployment in the 1930's. Full employment was brought by another unwelcome experience – War. Today's teenagers and older workers face a similarly uncertain future – but this time new solutions must be found.

Was there much unemployment where you lived in the 1930's? Did you or anyone in your family have to go far to look for work? Do you remember the Means Test?

Youth's revolt.
Each generation of young people makes its own statement about the world and the place they want in it.

When you were younger were there any special fashions which you and your friends took up? Do you remember the 'monkey parade' or 'monkey run'?

---

12 Man on the moon.
The unimaginable happened on July 20th, 1969 when we saw with our own eyes men actually walking on the moon!

What do you think is the most important achievement this century – nuclear power, space flight, computers, penicillin?

---

13 Steam train.
Clouds of steam surround the driver and fireman who might have time to notice their audience of admirers. Today's trains may not seem so hardworking or individual but the 125's and diesels have their loyal followers too.

What things do you remember about steam trains? Did you know anyone who worked on the railways? Was it a good sort of job to have?

---

14 Holidays – for all?
Cheaper travel and paid holidays have brought to many the undreamed luxury of holidays in exotic places. Majorca, Spain, Greece, Italy, North Africa have become almost as familiar as Blackpool, Minehead and Margate.

What was your first big holiday? Do you remember the first Holiday Camps? Did you ever take your children away on holiday?

---

15 Travelling by tram.
The old trams may not have travelled very fast but they were solid and dependable and forged their way defiantly through city traffic. Abroad, other Europeans can travel on a new generation of modern trams noted for their speed and silence.

Do you remember the turnaround seats on some trams? Did you travel to work by tram? Did you miss the trams when they went? What came in their place?

---

16 Traffic on the roads.
Lorries grow larger and heavier; their noise, speed and sheer size make them distressing to many people.

How did heavy traffic change the area you live in? How do you think the old and the young are affected by the lorries, cars and buses?

---

17 Cod liver oil on the National Health.
A national health service for each and all to ensure good health and an end to the deterrents of doctors' bills and costly medicines was set up in 1946. Children were to have a good start with free vitamins.

What happened if someone fell ill when you were young? Did your mother have her own remedies? How did people pay for the doctor and medicines? How did you feel when the National Health Service came in?

---

18 Hop picking.
Picking hops in the hop-gardens of Kent was a way of earning money and getting out into the countryside for some Londoners.

Did you or your family ever go hop picking or fruit picking? Where did you stay? How much were you paid? How did you travel there?

---

19 Family portrait.
There isn't much food to go round this large family and with so many to feed and clothe luxuries seem to be out of the question. Today a television set, washing machine and convenience foods help to knock off some of poverty's hard edges.

What stories did your grandparents tell you when you were young? How far back do they go? Did your grandparents help to look after you when you were young? Were there any old neighbours that you and your family knew well?

---

20 A different world.
Enormous changes in the lifetime of our oldest generation have transformed the world as we see it, although from the Apollo spaceship it still looks comfortingly as we imagined it. We reminisce through a radio telescope of time, enlightened by distance and reassured by the familiar.

What are the biggest changes you have seen in your life time? What do you think the young people of today have missed? In what ways do you consider that they are more fortunate than you were?

Notes

Reminiscence and old age

1 Charles N. Lewis: 'Reminiscing and self concept in old age', *Journal of Gerontology,* 1971, Vol. 26, 2.

2 Ibid.

3 Robert N. Butler: 'The life review: an interpretation of reminiscence in the aged', *Psychiatry,* 1963, Vol. 26, 1.

4 Ogden R. Lindsley: 'Geriatric behavioural prosthetics' in *New Thoughts on Old Age* Robert R. Kastenbaum (ed), New York, Springer, 1964. Arthur W. McMahon and Paul J. Rhudick:'Reminiscing in the aged: an adaptational response', *General Psychiatry,* 1964, 10.

5 James C. Folsom: 'Reality orientation for the elderly mental patient', *Journal of Geriatric Psychiatry,* 1968.

6 Una P. Holden and Alex Sinebruchow: 'Reality orientation therapy: a study investigating the value of this therapy in the rehabilitation of elderly people', *Age and Ageing,* 1978.

7 J. Sanbourne Bockoven: 'Aspects of geriatric care and treatment: Moral, amoral and immoral', in *Clinical Explorations.*

8 Paul Thompson: *The Voice of the Past,* Oxford University Press, 1978.

9 *Outreach Education and the Elders: theory and practice* Frank Glendenning (ed), Beth Johnson Foundation in association with the Department of Adult Education, University of Keele, 1980.

10 Edgar Miller: *Abnormal Ageing,* Wiley, London 1977.

The history of Recall

1 This chapter is largely based on the report of the project: *Reminiscence Aids: the use of audio-visual presentations to stimulate memories in old people with mental infirmity.* The report may be consulted in the D.H.S.S. Library, Alexander Fleming House, Elephant & Castle, London S.E.1.

2 For the Reminiscence Aids team: June 1978-August 1979, please see page 3.

3 Slide/tape was selected as a medium because of its flexibility – the images could be held on the screen for as long as desired and the slides and tape could be used independently of each other.

4 For members of the Advisory Committee: June 1978-August 1979, please see page 3.

5 Mr. Edward Baker.

6 The testing programme was devised by Mick Kemp and Rowan Matthews. A full account of the procedure may be read in the report of the project.

7 Ian Breakwell worked on the project by arrangement with The Artists' Placement Group (Research) Ltd. as did two other members of the team, Hugh Davies and David Toop.

8 *Community Care* 8/1978 *Mind Out,* 30 9/1978 *Observer* 12/11/78 *NRC Handelsbaad* (in Dutch) 6/1/79 *Toronto Star* 10/3/79 *Doctor Magazine* 22/3/79 *Daily Mail* 29/3/79 *The Washington Post* 3/1979 *London Police Pensioner* 6/11/79

9 *Radio London* 6/1978 *Woman's Hour* 1/1979

10 *Getting On* (ATV) 8/7/1979

Using Recall

1 The presentation lasted 15-20 minutes and contained approximately 60 slides. Although the slide sequence was punctuated at intervals by dark slides, it was still beyond the capacities of the severely demented. The pictures appeared too fleetingly on the screen to be assimilated and the spoken material hardly registered at all since it required a degree of concentration that these particular people no longer had.

2 'Reminiscence – a pilot study': Thelma Harvey and Rowena Kinsman (unpublished).

3 During June and July 1981 The London Boroughs' Training Committee (organising tutor Malcolm Ford) set up a series of six training sessions on the use of *Recall.* These were well attended by people working in social services training departments, residential homes, day centres, hospitals etc.

4 At a meeting of the Association of Teachers in Community Education (Community Service Volunteers) *Recall* was shown and as a result some pupils at Sevenoaks School worked on a slide/tape sequence on the Second World War, using the reminiscences of local residents.

Developing Recall

1 'Sweet sixteen' was an idea arising out of a community project for Town and Country Inter-Action (Milton Keynes) Ltd. A description of the project may be found in *A Report October '75 - May '78 Town and Country Inter-Action (Milton Keynes) Ltd,* Inter-Action, 15 Wilkin Street, London NW5 3NG.

Suggested reading

Reminiscence and old age

Robert N. Butler
'The life review: an interpretation of reminiscence in the aged', *Psychiatry*, 1963, Vol. 26, 1.

Robert J. Havighurst and Richard Glasser
'An exploratory study of reminiscence', *Journal of Gerontology* 1972, Vol. 27, 2.

Mick Kemp and Rowan Matthews
'Managing psychogeriatric problems', *Geriatric Medicine*, June 1979, Vol. 9, 6.

Charles N. Lewis
'Reminiscing and self concept in old age', *Journal of Gerontology*, 1971, Vol. 26, 2.

Arthur W. McMahon and Paul J. Rhudick
'Reminiscing in the aged: an adaptational response', *General Psychiatry*, 1964, 10.

Andrew Norris and Mohammed T.R. Abu El Eileh
'Reminiscence groups: a therapy for both elderly patients and their staff', (to be published)

General reading

D.B. Bromley
The Psychology of Human Ageing, Penguin, 1974

Erik Erikson
Childhood and Society, Hogarth Press, 1963

I.M.C. Hunter
Memory, Penguin, 1964

Edgar Miller
Abnormal Ageing, Wiley, 1977

George Miller
Psychology: the Science of Mental Life, Penguin, 1968

Paul Thompson
The Voice of the Past, Oxford University Press, 1974

Illustrated books

Susan Briggs
Keep Smiling Through, Weidenfeld & Nicholson, 1977

Harold Chapman
Down Memory Lane, Dent, 1980

John Gorman
To Build Jerusalem, Scorpion, 1980

James Howgego
London in the Twenties and Thirties, Batsford, 1978

Dennis Judd
The Life and Times of George V, Weidenfeld & Nicholson, 1973

Billy Kay (ed)
Odyssey: Voices from Scotland's Past, Polygon, 1980

C.S. Makepeace
Lancashire in the Twenties and Thirties, Batsford, 1977

Arthur Marwick
Women at War, 1914-1918, Fontana, 1977

Raynes Minns
Bombers and Mash: The Domestic Front, 1939-45, Virago, 1980

Sallie Purkis (ed)
Into the Past (series), Longmans, 1980

Paul Thompson and Gina Harkell
The Edwardians in Photographs, Batsford, 1979

Victorian and Edwardian . . . (series) Includes volumes on counties and regions, transport, army, children, country topics, farming, crime and punishment. Batsford

Gordon Winter
A Cockney Camera, Penguin, 1975

A Country Camera, Penguin, 1973

Addresses

Federation of Worker Writers and Community Publishers, 76 Carysfort Road, London N16.

Inter-Action,
15 Wilkin Street, London NW5 3NG.

Local Radio Workshop,
12 Praed Mews, London W2.

Manchester Studies,
Hilton House, Hilton Street, Manchester M1 2FE.

The Museums Association,
34 Bloomsbury Way, London WC1A 2SF.

Oral History Society,
Department of Sociology, University of Essex, Wivenhoe Park, Colchester, Essex CO4 3SQ.

Many local museums and libraries have collections of tapes, photographs and memorabilia which they may be willing to lend out or arrange as a short exhibition. Curators and libraries are usually interested to hear about reminiscence amongst older local residents and may offer helpful suggestions or welcome parties of visitors to their collections.